NINE DAYS IN PARIS
THE JOURNEY CONTINUES

NINE DAYS IN PARIS
THE JOURNEY CONTINUES

By
Warren Landrum

WARLAND BOOKS
GRAND PRAIRIE, TEXAS

NINE DAYS IN PARIS
Published by:
Warland Books
2791 Explorador
Grand Prairie, TX 75054
Warrenglandrum@hotmail.com

Warren Landrum, Publisher / Editorial Director
Carol Landrum, Photo Editor
Yvonne Rose/Quality Press, Production Coordinator

ALL RIGHTS RESERVED

No part of this book may be reproduced or transmitted in any form or by any means – electronic or mechanical, including photocopying, recording or by any information storage and retrieved system without written permission from the authors, except for the inclusion of brief quotations in a review.

Warland Books are available at special discounts for bulk purchases, sales promotions, fund raising or educational purposes.

© Copyright 2018 by WARREN LANDRUM and WARLAND Books

Paperback ISBN #: 978-0-9787355-5-5
Ebook ISBN #: 978-0-9787355-6-2
Library of Congress Control Number: 2018936343

DEDICATION

This book is dedicated to Paris, "The City of Lights." There is truly no other city in the world like You!

ACKNOWLEDGEMENTS

Even though my wife Carol did not feel that she contributed to this book enough to be credited as a co-author, it would not be what it is, without her taking this journey with me.

Thanks Boo!

TABLE OF CONTENTS

Dedication i

Acknowledgements iii

Introduction 1

Plan, Plan, Plan!! 5

T- 4 Days... 14

Thursday, June 8th 16

Bonus Time at Home 21

Take 2 25

Saturday, June 10th 29

Sunday, June 11th 37

Monday, June 12th 50

Tuesday, June 13th 58

Wednesday, June 14th 68

Carol's Birthday Dinner 84

Thursday, June 15th 88

Friday, June 16th 103

Saturday, June 17th 116

Sunday, June 18th 127

WRAP-UP 132

APPENDIX A 134

APPENDIX B 150

Street Artist Drawing of the Author — June 2017 151

Street Artist Drawing of the Author — 1997 152

Street Artist Drawing of the Author — New Year's Day, 1977 .. 153

About the Author 154

INTRODUCTION

I really didn't have a choice. After all of the positive feedback and responses that we received from the readers of *"Nine Days in Italy,"* this book HAD to happen. They literally implored me to capture the experiences and adventures that they knew we would have in Paris, and bring them to life within these pages, so that they could, once again, journey to Europe with us. Some of the readers had been to some of the same parts of Italy that we had, and they said that reading the book rekindled fond memories for them. Others said that they had never been over there, but it felt as though they were right there in the car and on the streets with us, experiencing every emotion right along with us. And still others said that they appreciated us laying out some of the things to be aware of (insider tips, if you will) in case they ever decide to travel to that part of the world. Thus, *"Nine Days in Paris: The Journey Continues"* is born.

    This was my third trip to Paris and my wife's first. It seems as though, since 1977, it has been my destiny to be in Paris every 20 years. I first visited in 1977 when I was in the

1

United States Air Force, stationed at Bitburg Air Base in Germany. On that occasion, I went over on a bus with a bunch of my Air Force buddies and it was quite an adventure. We actually got there a few days before New Year's Day 1977, and thus had the opportunity to experience New Year's Eve and the transition in Paris. And what an experience it was! I remember being in a restaurant a few minutes before midnight, and then at the stroke of midnight, everyone busted out into the streets from wherever they were, and people just started grabbing and kissing each other all over. It was madness! The crowd was so dense that I got separated from my buddies and I actually spent the rest of the night on my own going from Metro stop to Metro stop, just hopping off to try to find someone to party with, at whichever stop I wound up at. I guess I was too young and stupid to be afraid. The 40-year-old me probably would not have been as quick to train-hop all alone as the 22-year-old me was!

At one of the stops, I wound up partying with some guys from Northern Africa for a while. They looked like someone you might see in "Ali Baba and The Forty Thieves" with their turbans and such. I vaguely remember some of them even had those big cutlasses that they carried in the cartoons!

When I got back to my hotel (luckily, I had a book of matches on me with the name of the hotel on it) about 10am, after partying through the night, my buddies and the bus had already left for Germany. I had about 40 Francs (10 US Dollars) in my pocket at the time, so all I could do was poke around until I found another little hotel that I could afford until the next morning (Monday), at which time I went to the US Embassy, and they provided me a train ticket back to my base in Germany. When I got back to the base, the guys said that they had been toasting me on the bus all the way back, because they thought for sure, they would never see me again!

My 2nd trip to Paris, 20 years later in 1997, was more conventional, and less adventurous. I went over as part of a team for the semiconductor company that I worked for at the time. We were rolling out new computer systems all over Europe, at the company's offices in Reading, England; Milan, Paris, and Munich. Paris was our third stop. What I remember most about Paris during that short three-day stay was going to the Louvre museum and spending about 3-4 hours just studying ONE painting. The painting was huge, covering an entire wall that must have been at least half-a-football field long. As you progressed in the painting from left to right, it told a story. It was truly amazing, and I think that's when I first began to appreciate the fact that some of the artists that I had read about in the history books, really WERE artistic masters and geniuses.

So now, here we are 20 years later in 2017, and I'm off to Paris again. As I said, it must be my destiny and I could not wait to see what new adventures and experiences awaited. Since I was going as a married man this time, accompanied by my wife, I had no doubt the experience would have a totally different perspective.

I had serious trepidations about writing a book that was pre-planned. Most of the things that I have written, whether short stories, or articles, or my other books, came from some type of inspiration and, for the most part, were more or less spontaneous. So, I feared that I would lose some of that spontaneity going into a trip with a pre-conceived goal. *Nine Days in Italy* had most definitely been born of the moment.

After all of the adventures that we experienced in our FIRST DAY on that trip, I knew that our time there was going to be something out of the ordinary. So, I started jotting down notes of that first day's highs and lows on that first night to lay the groundwork for the story that begged to be told. We made time to do that every night on the trip, and we were so excited and so wanting to capture the story while it was still fresh in our minds, we actually completed the writing of the book within one month after our return, and the book was published less than two months after that. Boy, talkin' 'bout hot off the press!

As I sit here in my office writing this brief introduction, we are still 15 days away from boarding our plane at DFW Airport in Dallas and making that 3-hour flight to Dulles in Washington D.C., before we take that final 7.5-hour leg into Charles de Gaulle International Airport outside of Paris. Of course, preparation is the key to maximizing the fun and enjoyment quotient on any vacation, so we (or should I say I, since I am the Self-Proclaimed Family Entertainment and Fun Director) have pretty much got our daily itinerary all laid out. But, we'll get to that in a moment. I want to tell you a bit first about some of the basic preliminary prep that is vital for any international trip. I say basic, and I am not trying to insult the intelligence of some of you who may be more seasoned, experienced travelers, but I want to make sure that I convey to anyone who may not be so well-versed in travel, or at least international travel, some of the things that may easily be forgotten or possibly overlooked. So, I invite you to buckle up and strap yourselves in as you prepare to join us on this, somewhat bumpy, but ultimately wonderful adventure we had on our trek through Paris!

PLAN, PLAN, PLAN!!

Let's start with The Passport. In regard to the Passport, first of all, make sure you have one – DOH! I knew that we had ours, so the next thing to do is to double-check the expiration date to make sure it will still be valid during the dates of your trip. And make this check far enough in advance so that you will have ample time to obtain or renew your passport without having to try and scramble to get this done within days of your departure date. Who wants or needs the unnecessary sweat or headache that forgetting to do this basic, but vital, task ahead of time could cause. I know I sure don't!

As I mentioned earlier, the key to getting the most out of any vacation is planning. I know that some people like to go on vacations that are totally unplanned and unstructured, where they just ride the waves of the moment and let the trip unfold in whatever shape or form it takes. I'm okay with that, and on some trips and some vacations, I do that myself, at least to some degree, if not totally. But when I am spending the kind of airfare money it takes to get to Paris, and I know, from experience, that nine days on the ground is really not a whole lot of time, based on the endless plethora of things there are to see and do in Paris, I plan!

There are a few different categories that you can get into in regard to planning for the trip. They are:
1. Plan based on Personal Experience, if you have been to the locale before.
2. Research.
3. Talk to Folks.

Let me tell you a little bit about what I did in each of these categories to maximize our preparation. Before I do though, let me tell you that you can *feel free to skip over this section and go directly to the Chapter labeled "Saturday, June 10th, on page 31, which starts with our landing at Charles de Gaulle Airport in France, if you'd like.* But I guarantee you that if you stick with me and complete this section, it will add tons of enjoyment to your trip, especially if you maybe decide to use some of the same or similar types of research methodology. I know, I know, you're saying, "Research! What does this idiot think we want to do – prepare for a College Exam or something?"

I promise you, that's the furthest thing from my mind. Just keep this thought in your head as you go forward – Maximize the Experience! This could be taken two ways – maximize your experience in reading this book and getting your money's worth, or Maximizing the Experience should this book stimulate you enough to get on over to Paris for the first time (or even to revisit it again, because you KNOW you didn't do everything you wanted to the last time you were there!) Anyhow, your choice. Now, where was I? Oh yeah... Plan, Plan, Plan!!

Plan based on Personal Experience, if you have been to the locale before

As I mentioned earlier, I have had the opportunity of experiencing Paris twice before. So, between those two trips to Paris, I already had a pretty good lay of the land. I had visited some of the major attractions, like The Louvre, with Mona Lisa, and the Eiffel Tower and Arc de Triomphe and had strolled down the Champs-Elysees. I had hung out in Montmartre, visiting Sacre-Couer (the Basilica of the Sacred Heart) and I knew how to get around on the Metro rail system. So, I felt pretty good about what I already knew. I just wanted to do more research to try to make sure that Carol got to experience all of the major attractions, and that we were both able to experience some that I had not been to on my previous travels. We wanted to Maximize the Experience and I had no doubt that we would!

Research

This was going to be the fun, yet tedious and painstaking part. Fortunately, I am a detail-oriented person (some would say anal ☺), so digging into things to find answers is right up my ballywick. My research would take two paths – Printed Materials and Online Internet Research. Here's what I did in both those areas:

- *Printed Materials*

The first thing I did here was to look in my personal library. Lo and behold, I came across a copy of *"The Complete Idiot's Guide to Planning Your Trip to Europe."* Even though my copy was almost 20 years old, I still came across something I did not know, that would prove useful as I did further research down the road. The piece of info was simply that, when looking at the address of a place, whether it be a tourist destination or restaurant, or your hotel or whatever, the last two digits in the Zip Code tells you what arrondissement the place is in. Paris is divided into 20 of these arrondissements, spiraling out from the 1st one, which includes The Louvre. It is important to know which of these districts each entity is in, when you are planning the logistics of what you want to see, so that you can kind of group things that are closer together into the same day's viewing. A small piece of info like that will pay huge dividends.

I knew that we would be doing a lot of walking in Paris, so on one of my trips to my favorite store, Barnes and Noble, I went over to their travel section and started looking at the books and guides about Paris. I found a perfect little handbook that was put together by National Geographic, which was entitled *"Walking Paris, The Best of The City: A Step-By-Step Guide."* As I paged through this little book, I could tell it would be just what I needed. It broke its chapters down into sections by Neighborhood or arrondissement, and it highlighted all of the major attractions, in addition to having great info on some places that I was not familiar with. And it had great color photographs, as well. This was a nice compact (5" x 7") little guidebook, and I could easily carry it along with us as we traveled through the city.

- *On the Internet*

Of course, we all know that there is so much information about EVERYTHING out on the Internet, that we could easily get lost up in there and spend the rest of our lives Surfing the Net, if we aren't careful! But with a little focus, and with Google as your Best Friend, you can find useful info relatively quick.

After a few minutes of Googling "Paris," I came across something called the Paris Pass. After reading about it, and already having in my mind some of the things that I wanted us to do on our trip, this started to sound more and more like a good deal. It was a little pricey, but when I started adding up all the costs of all things that I wanted to do, and compared the prices of purchasing them individually, as opposed to buying this Paris Pass, the Paris Pass won. Of course, it is only cost-effective, if you are going to use it a lot. Let me break down some of the main components:

1. It lets you get into about 60 of the museums around Paris for free, and lets you go to the "Front of the line" at The Louvre. As we found out in our trip to Italy last year, these "Skip The Line" passes are well worth the money in regards to time-saving, because you can easily spend 1 or 2 hours in line at major attractions.
2. Gets you into places like The Arc de Triomphe and Notre Dame free.
3. Free Seine River Cruise.
4. Free entrance to Palace of Versailles
5. Big Bus, Hop On, Hop Off – where you can take tours around the city, hopping off at about 12 different major attractions to check them out.
6. Unlimited use of the Metro (train) and Bus transportation in the city (this is HUGE).

Limitations:

1. Does not include entry into the Eiffel Tower, which is probably one of the Top 2 attractions in the City
2. You can get a 4 or 6-day Paris Pass, and it starts from when you first use one of the features. So, if you are going to be in town for more than 6 days, you have to figure out when you want to start using it to maximize your benefit/ROI.

The Internet is also useful for checking out more info about some of the places you want to visit to get things like the days that they are not open, Hours of Admission, addresses and things like that. One of the sites I definitely recommend is VIATOR.COM. They have a wealth of places and sites of interest to check out, and they have great details of the sites, in addition to reviews by those who have purchased tickets from them. I have purchased Viator events pre-trip for both land-based vacations such as this Paris trip, and also for excursions when taking cruises.

And of course, one of the FIRST things you will probably use the Internet for is to Book your Trip. We used Orbitz.com and found a package deal that included Air and a nice little hotel close to the Montmartre District, which is a great artsy district only about 15-20 minutes' walk from The Louvre (or so they say).

Talking to Folks
1. **Niece of a Friend of ours at a Crawfish Boil at the friend's house.**

    She had been to Paris before and gave us a tip about the Black Paris Walking Tours. I Googled that and found some of them that were offered and honed in on what turned out to be the main and best one in my opinion – Ricki Stevenson's Black Paris Walking Tour. Ricki is an ex-pat from the Oakland, California area originally, and she started her tours back in 1993. I'll talk about some of our experiences gained during the tour in one of the chapters, but it promises to be quite the deal, giving insights and tips not only about the "Black" experience in Paris, but also good Restaurant and Jazz Club tips as well, among other useful tidbits of data.

2. **Mayor Ron Jensen of Grand Prairie, Texas**

    I was talking to Mayor Jensen in the City's Suite at the Verizon Theatre during intermission of a John Legend concert that he had given us tickets to (Sidebar – this was the best concert/production I have seen in the last 40 years. If you get a chance to see John Legend, do it!), and knowing that he had been to Paris a few times, I asked him to give me some tips about anything off the beaten path that I may not know about. Well, he asked me if my wife Carol liked gardens. I told him that she did, and he told me that the Monet Gardens outside of town were quite beautiful and she might enjoy that experience. The site was the home of French

Impressionist painter Claude Monet and was the location where he actually did a lot of his paintings from, and of. Going there would also give us a day-trip outside of Paris proper, with a chance to see some of the French countryside. Carol was also familiar with Monet from an Art Appreciation class she had taken a few years ago, while getting here Bachelor's in Nursing; so that would make this excursion even more meaningful. I looked up the Monet Gardens and booked our reservation that very night as soon as I got home from the concert!

Putting it All Together

So, after recalling all of your past experiences about the place, and doing your research, and talking to folks, you are ready to tackle putting together your personal itinerary. But let me mention one more essential planning item before I get into the itinerary.

I was sitting at my desk at work 15 days out from our departure date, when the phone rang. It was my wife. She said that she was at Ross, the clothing store, to pick up a few pieces of clothing for the trip, and she was wondering what the weather was going to be like over there while we were there. DOH! The one thing I had forgotten. I just kinda figured that Paris in June would be pretty nice, I had not even bothered to check the historical forecast for the dates we would be there, let alone the current forecast. I told my wife I'd check it out and call her right back. Luckily, as I said, we were within 15 days, so I was able to get a current short-term forecast when I got online and found that the range was basically going to be a high of around 77 going down to around 58 or 59 in the evenings. So, I called my wife back with this info, and she continued on her errand to start the vacation drain on our bank account. But let me share a little secret with you here. Shhhh!

I had seen something on Facebook roughly a year before our departure date, and before we even decided that we would be in Paris. It was a Savings suggestion, where the deal was to do 52-weeks of savings where you would put $1 in on Week 1, $2 in on Week 2 and so on, all the way up to $52 in Week 52. So, as it turns out, we will be in Week 47 when our plane leaves from DFW Airport, with each of us having $1128 in our "Piggy Banks." With that knowledge in mind, I just smiled and gave a little nod at the thought of Carol shopping at Marshall's. You gotta love it ☺!!!

Now back to the Itinerary. I'm not going to bore you here by laying out the Itinerary in detail, because it will all be revealed, once we actually start the trip; and I KNOW that some of the things I have planned will change once we get into the trip, and it starts taking on a life of its own. The main goal of the itinerary is just to lay out some of the major attractions you want to see, to make sure you don't miss them. But you have to be flexible.

Suffice to say, I was able to use all of the research data collected to lay out what I thought was the most efficient plan for Maximizing our Fun. So now, the hardest part of the vacation begins – waiting these last two weeks until we actually get on that plane.

See ya in a couple of weeks!!!

T- 4 DAYS...

Well, it's Sunday, June 4th and we leave Thursday, the 8th. Carol is finally starting to show some excitement. 'Bout time!

We are getting down to the real nitty-gritty now. I had to go up to the attic and bring down the suitcases we would be using, as we started going through our closets, picking out which clothes we were going to take. It was time for an updated 4-15-day weather check to see how that earlier forecast was holding up. Looks like the first couple of days will be around 5 degrees warmer than the last forecast, pushing up into the low 80's; but after that it was pretty much as predicted, with daytime highs around 75-77, getting down to around the mid-50's at night. So now we knew exactly which clothes to pick.

It was also time to re-look at the itinerary and fine-tune it as much as possible, making sure that we took care of as many of the little logistic details that could bite you as possible. The main thing here was to review the suggestions from the Black Paris Walking Tour (BPWT) information that they had sent to us in a PDF file and take that into consideration with what we knew we wanted to do from the Paris Pass, to tighten things up.

I also called the credit card companies of the two cards I would be taking to alert them of the dates that we would be using the cards overseas so that they would not put a fraud stop on cards. Additionally, you may be able to prevent having foreign rates or fees put on your transactions by calling them beforehand

With these final tasks done, I felt that we were finally all set to go and there was nothing left but to wait for Departure Day, June 8th.

THURSDAY, JUNE 8ᵀᴴ

Trumped at the Airport

Before I go on with this recounting of our adventures, I'd like to take a step back and put some context on our trip, in regard to what was going on in the world, and specifically the United States, during the time of our trip. I think that it is important to the reader to get some idea about this, especially since some of the goings-on specifically affected the outcome of our trip. It would also put into context a bit of what it was like to be an American traveling over to Europe during this particular time in our nation's history.

As any of you that were attuned to the political climate in the United States are aware, during the first half of 2017, coinciding with the time period from President Donald Trump's inauguration in January, through mid-June, there was an air of political unrest and uncertainty in the United States; as we tried to get used to Trump as President and as our Congress and the FBI conducted investigations to determine if any members of the Trump Presidential

Campaign had colluded with the Russians to influence our 2016 Presidential elections; and whether or not President Trump was guilty of Obstruction of Justice, an impeachable offense, in trying to take measures from preventing the investigations from going forward. The potential scandal and cover-up(s) that were possibly being unearthed by the never-ending stream of disclosures and leaks from sources within the government, were proving to be possibly bigger than the Watergate Cover-up and Scandal that led to President Richard Nixon's impeachment and resignation in the 1970's.

On the morning that we were to leave for Paris, the former Director of the FBI, James Comey, was scheduled to testify before a Senate Intelligence oversight committee to give an account of his interactions and meetings with President Trump, some of which ultimately led to his being fired by Trump. The buildup for and to this testimony was huge, and I had programmed our television to record all of his testimony and the ensuing analysis that would be done on TV by the "Talking Heads" for the remainder of that day. I planned on reviewing this when we got back from Paris. I must admit, I was fascinated by what was unfolding.

We got to the airport and went through security and were at our gate, E37, about an hour-and-a-half before the time we were scheduled to board our plane. As on our trip to Italy a few months earlier, we had been selected for Pre-Select, meaning we got to go to a shorter line and did not have to take off our shoes or belts, greatly streamlining the security process. So, we, mostly I, proceeded to find some seats close to one of the TV Monitors that were broadcasting Comey's testimony and settled in to watch as much as we could before Boarding Call. Our flight was scheduled to leave at 11:50, which meant we should start boarding around 11:20.

At around 11:30, I noticed that our boarding call had not been issued and I did not see any activity around our gate. I pulled out my ticket to check the info again and saw that we were supposed to be at gate E27, not E37! We had about 10 minutes to get there!

We quickly started fast-walking back toward E27. When we got to a fork in the hallway, we saw that we had to hang a right. We did and within a few yards, I saw that there was an escalator that would carry us down one level. We got on the escalator, and halfway down, we saw that it was going down another level, and when we reached the bottom, we saw that there was a moving sidewalk that stretched for maybe a couple of hundred yards in front of us, leading to another building. *We are toast*, I thought, but started running at this point, hoping to get lucky and get to the gate before the door was closed. No such luck. The gate was the first one on the left as I got to the top of the escalator; but as soon as I saw it, I also saw the empty ticket counter, and no agent at the walkway door, and the door was locked. "Rats!" I ran over to the agent at the next gate and asked if she could call somebody and tell them we were out there, but she said it was too late, as the runway had probably already been pulled back.

I ran back to the gate and started banging on the window, hoping that the workers that I saw out there would hear me. The chocks had not been pulled back yet. I spotted the pilot, and I could see him going through his final checks, but he could not see me. Obviously, he was not even looking in my direction.

Thursday, June 8th

I then started pounding and pounding on the door as loud as I could, yelling "Open up!" No response. My wife told me later that I was lucky that security had not passed by at that time, or they would have arrested me as a madman and security threat or something. I remember looking back at the half-dozen or so passengers that were waiting for the next flight out of that gate, and they were either just looking at me with no emotion, or not even paying attention seemingly. Bizarre. I started pounding again.

Finally, after about three or four more minutes, some of the workers pulled the chocks away, and the aircraft started backing out. We were officially toast! I went over and talked to an agent at another gate, and he said that we would have to wait for the agent from our gate to come back down the runway, so we could see if he could help us. Long story short, after lamenting and sympathizing with us, he was able to book us on the same flight the next morning. So, we would lose one day out of our trip. But at least, he rebooked us at no charge. I guess there's always a bright side ☹. One item worth noting here is that, although we missed the flight, our luggage did not, and was merrily on its way to Dulles airport in Washington D.C., even as we were rebooking with the agent. My wife was taking all of this surprisingly well, which surprised me because when things go wrong like this, she is usually getting on my case about what I did wrong to get us into the situation at hand. But she just said that all things happen for a reason, so maybe The Lord was just trying to slow us down or something, and maybe we were not supposed to be in Paris just yet. I guess that's a philosophical way to look at it, but all I could feel was anger at myself, for being so obsessed with that testimony on that screen, that I did not handle my business.

I had been Trumped…!

Oh yeah, by the way, we had to take a cab to get home, since our daughter was at work, and the cabbie ripped us off, charging us $64 for a trip that, the last time we took a cab from the airport, cost about $35. He must have added another $10 or $20 to the tab when he pulled into the driveway and saw how large the house was, and I was just too frustrated at myself to even put up a fight!

BONUS TIME AT HOME

When I woke up to the sound of the alarm clock on Friday, the first thing I heard was the sound of the raindrops pounding against the gutter pipe. This rainstorm would prove to be a not-insignificant event. Before I go any further though, let me recap the fallout that resulted from our missing our flight out of Dallas on the previous day.

On the negative side, I had to make a few phone calls and update people on what was happening as a result of the missed flight. This was really not so much a negative, as an inconvenience that had to be attended to.

First, and most importantly of all, I had to call our hotel in Paris to inform them of our new arrival time and day to make sure we still had a room to stay in when we got there. After looking up the international dialing instructions for the U.S. to Paris, I got them with no problem. They informed me that they would not be able to credit me for the night lost, but otherwise, no problem – the room was all ours whenever we arrived. Check!

Next, I sent an e-mail to the founder and operator of our Black Paris Walking Tour, Ricki Stevenson, and informed her that we had missed our flight and we would be arriving in Paris at 6:55am on the day that our tour with her was scheduled. I told her that we would be too tired to really enjoy the tour and asked if we could reschedule it for either Sunday or Monday. Ricki got back to me relatively quickly and told me that she had re-booked us for Monday. She told me that it would take us 3 or 4 hours to get through Customs and the procedures at Charles de Gaulle Airport, so there was no way we would have made the 10am tour start time. She told us to just rest up and recoup on Saturday after we arrived, and she would see us on Monday. Check!

The final thing I had to do was to get into the Super Shuttle app on my cell phone and change the arrival day from June 9th to June 10th. The app allowed me to do this with no problem, so we were now all set.

On the positive side, the missed flight and rebooking meant that Carol and I would get to spend an extra day with our granddaughter, Mia. Mia would stay with us all day and night until our daughter picked us up at 8:30am on Friday to take us back to the airport.

Mia took full advantage of her 'bonus' time with Nana and Papa. She first convinced Nana to let her come out into the back yard to help her water the plants and flowers. All was going well until Carol gave Mia the hose and told her to "make it rain" by making a shower over the pool. Mia complied – at first – squirting the water out over the pool and into the air, pointing the hose upward to make it rain as directed. But soon, she got the bright idea to turn the hose toward Nana and me. She caught us off-guard and lightly soaked us as we ran around the corner of the house to try to get away from her. But this was a problem, as we could not afford to lose sight of her, with the pool so close to her. But as we peeked around to make sure we could keep her in sight, she spotted us and really blasted us this time! We were soaked so badly that I had to immediately take off my shirt. I raced toward her to try and grab the hose, while Carol headed inside to try and dry her now wet-and-frazzled hair. I successfully snatched the hose out of Mia's hands, as she squealed like a little happy piglet, and that ended that episode.

Later that day, Carol took Mia shopping with her as she picked up a couple of items of clothing at Marshall's for the trip.

Mia had been telling us how she wanted a green flute to play. Not just ANY flute, mind you, but a GREEN one! Well, I was surprised and overjoyed when they returned from the store. Mia ran into the house with a box, telling me that Nana had got the green flute for her. Sure enough, I opened the box and it contained four items:

1. A green flute
2. A xylophone
3. A tambourine and
4. 2 cymbals

After we unpacked these items, Mia began assigning roles to everyone. She took the flute for herself and gave me the xylophone and Carol the tambourine. Each started playing our instruments, following her directions, and the Mia Band was born!

So, all this added up to an exhausting, pre-departure 'bonus' to our vacation. Instead of a lazy day flying across the Atlantic, we had a water-adventure-and-Mia's-Band day extra-bonding time with our beautiful granddaughter. Who could ask for anything more!

TAKE 2

Back at the airport – Friday Morning

We arrived back at the airport at about 9:30 for our 11:50 flight. After munching on some bagel and egg sandwiches from Einstein's and some coffee and tea from Starbucks, we settled into some seats at our gate to await our boarding call. But this time, I checked to make sure we were at the correct gate!

At around 11 o'clock, about 20 minutes prior to the start of boarding, I checked with the gate agent to make sure everything was going as scheduled. To my surprise and dismay, he told me that because of severe weather, our flight departure had been delayed for almost an hour, and we would get into Dulles in Washington DC, at about 5:15pm. Our connecting flight to Paris was scheduled to leave at about 5:25, so there was no way we were going to make it.

The agent told me to go check with another United agent about three gates over to see if she could get me re-routed to Paris. I walked over to that gate and the agent told me she would be with me in a minute after she got logged in. When she was finally ready, I explained our situation to her. She understood and told me she could re-route us through O'Hare in Chicago with a plane leaving from this gate at 12:47pm. She said that would put us into Paris at about 9:30 the next morning, about 2.5 hours later than we were scheduled to arrive. Not having much choice, I told her to go ahead and do it.

She then checked on our bags and saw that they were still in Dulles in DC. They could not transfer them to an international flight, since we had not been on the flight with them the previous day. She told us that the bags should be in Paris though, when we arrived the next day. So, we were good to go… or so we thought.

O'Hare Field – Chicago

Our brief 3-4-hour layover at O'Hare was uneventful. I was again reminded of how huge this airport was as we went from our arrival gate to our departure gate, passing through the hub of the terminals. There was a long moving sidewalk connecting us from Concourse C to the main Concourse B of Terminal 1, and we were treated to a laser light show as we progressed along that sidewalk. When we reached the B Concourse and turned left toward our gate, we entered a long hallway. The first thing that you noticed was this huge dinosaur skeleton, that of a Brachiosauraus, which has been on loan to the airport from the Field Museum of Natural History, since 2016.

Take 2

Also standing out were the flags of the various nations that adorned the ceiling heights of this structure. And last but not least, as you make that left turn and looked to the right, just before the dinosaur, you see the Garrett's Popcorn stand. Garrett's is an institution for Chicagoans, and anyone who has tasted the Garret Mix is hooked for life. So, of course I had to stop there, and get a Medium bag to take on the plane with us.

We proceeded along the concourse and found our gate, and then doubled back to the Food Court we had passed to have a nice Mexican dinner before we boarded. Enjoying the statues representing some of Chicago's jazz music greats as we dined, we sat back and relaxed, before finishing up and walking over to our gate. Within 30 minutes we got our boarding call, and 20 minutes later, we were airborne, headed for Paris!

SATURDAY, JUNE 10TH

Charles de Gaulle Airport

We arrived at Charles de Gaulle (CDG) Airport about 31 minutes ahead of schedule, at 8:45am on Saturday, June 10th. We were in row 30 (out of 46) of a big Boeing 777-200 aircraft, so it took us around 20-25 minutes just to deplane. CDG Airport had a layout getting off the planes unlike any I had ever seen before in regard to the jetways. They had a series of escalators that took you from the jetways to the terminals and we could see the ones from other gates in kind of a criss-crossing pattern enclosed in tubes on various levels once we got on ours. The walking surfaces on these escalators were a really bouncy type of rubber. It was kind of futuristic, just like something you would see in an old Jetsons cartoon episode.

We quickly passed through Passport Control with no issues and went off searching for Baggage Services so that we could reclaim our luggage, which was supposed to already be here. We followed the signs and easily found Baggage Services. But our joy immediately turned into dismay and disappointment, when, after telling the agent our story, she took our Baggage Receipts from us, and verified that our bags would not arrive until the next day. Apparently, they had not been able to leave from Dulles the prior day, since we had not yet been confirmed as passengers on an international flight to Paris, due to the weather delay and subsequent re-routing to Chicago that we had experienced as a result of the weather. She was able to verify that our bags had been scanned, but she gave us some paperwork to fill out and told us that our bags would be delivered to our hotel room the next morning. Armed – and somewhat depleted – with this latest piece of info, we sucked it up, and headed on to our next mission – tracking down the pre-booked Super Shuttle driver who was to take us to our hotel.

As we left the Baggage Service area and entered the main area on this level of the terminal, we saw a booth that looked like an information desk and decided to stop there to ask if they knew where to pick up the Super Shuttle van. The young man there spoke a little English and told us we needed to catch the elevator down to the lower level to catch our ride. We did so, and got down there, and followed the signs to where we thought we should be. After about 15 minutes or so, and not seeing anything looking like Super Shuttle, my wife asked another person who looked "official" and HE told us that we needed to go back upstairs and out to Entry 24. We did this and still no luck. So, I decided to go back inside, and this time, we actually saw a booth that said Tourist Information. I talked to the young lady, and she pointed to a phone on the desk, and said that we should use it to actually call our Super Shuttle driver to let him know we had arrived. The phone was actually labeled "Super

Shuttle" and had the phone number to call, so I felt that we had finally talked to the right person. I reached Super Shuttle and told them who we were, and they said our driver would be there in about 15 or 20 minutes. They told us he would meet us by Entry 24. We went back to Entry 24 and there was a covered Bus Stop right across from it. An official of the bus companies asked us if we needed a bus into Paris. We told him we were just waiting for our Super Shuttle ride and he told us, we could wait right inside the bus stop. We did and around 30 minutes later, the driver found us and led us and the other people he was picking up on a circuitous path upstairs and downstairs and up one elevator and down another to, it seems like, right where we started almost. But after about 10 minutes of wandering around like lost sheep, we finally reached the van. Hallelujah!

When we got in the van, there was already one single lady and one couple in it. With the addition of us new arrivals, that made four parties that would be sharing this vehicle on our ride into Paris. We settled into the back seat with the single woman and we were off. It was right around High Noon.

Paris – At Last!

It was actually a pretty interesting ride into Paris, primarily because the young lady who had gotten on the shuttle with us, along with her mother, turned out to be quite interesting. She was probably in her 20's and had recently completed a 2-year Peace Corps assignment in Togo, Africa. She recounted some of her experiences over there, including the fact that she was paid just $1.75 USD per day while over there. But she said that it was such a poor country, that that was more than enough to suffice.

As luck would have it, we were the last ones to get dropped off, so it took us about two hours to get to our hotel, the Hotel Cyrnos Opera. But that was okay, because we got our first look at some of Paris's iconic landmarks on the way, such as the Seine River, the Eiffel Tower, The Musee de Orsay, and the Arc de Triomphe.

The Hotel Cyrnos Opera was a typical, quaint little Parisian hotel. It was located in the middle of a city block and had 23 rooms spread over seven floors. Our room was on the 3rd floor and that floor had four rooms on it. There was one elevator that was barely large enough to carry both of us up. Of course, since we did not have any luggage at this point, we did not have to worry about squeezing our bags in on the elevator!

The room was also a bit small, compared to American hotel rooms, but that was okay. Just like when you're on a cruise ship, the room was pretty much just a place to shower and sleep and change clothes to hit the street again. Our room did have a nice view though. Looking to the left, you could get a view of the typical 5-story Parisian apartment buildings that lined most of the streets of Paris. We will give more about the history of these buildings a little later. Looking directly across the street, you were looking at a side street, and could see how, directly behind the apartment building that fronted it, it veered off at an angle to another side street. This was typical of the way the streets were designed. The apartment building directly across from us had a Fresh Fruit store on the end of it, and right next door was a small restaurant/bar that was typical Parisian, with some small tables and chairs out front, so that the patrons/diners could sit and watch the parade of people go by. As we found out throughout our time over there, this was a favorite past-time of both the locals and tourists.

It did not take us too long to get settled into our room, since we did not have our luggage yet. Surprisingly, we weren't that tired or sleepy, so we decided to go for a walk and explore the neighborhood around our hotel. So, we went back downstairs and decided to make a left as we exited the front door of our new home-for-a week, and stepped onto our street, rue Montmartre. It was Saturday afternoon by this time, probably around 1pm or so. The streets were filled with people. As we walked along, all you could see on both sides of the street were those big five-story buildings that seemed to be on every street and took up the entire block. We walked for a couple of blocks and passed some fruit markets and bakeries, and of course, a few cafes and restaurants. After a few blocks, we got to what seemed to be a major intersection where about five streets came together.

We would find out later that this was pretty common. So, we decided to cross the street and take the right fork, as there appeared to be an interesting-looking large church looming ahead of us a few hundred yards.

The church turned out to be *Eglise St.-Eustache,* an unfinished masterpiece of Gothic architecture. Construction on it had started in 1532 and it took over 100 years to build. Famous composers like Liszt and Berlioz had performed there, and it has an 8000-pipe organ, which is among Paris' largest.

As we got right opposite the church at the end of the block, the area opened up into a giant street-market type deal. There were vendors peddling all sorts of wares – clothing, toys, books, you name it. There was a large open cobblestone piazza just beyond the vendors; and looking to the left, we saw the building that seemed to be comprised of a huge array of multi-colored tubes. You couldn't miss this building and it was one we had passed a couple of times as our driver was delivering us to our hotel that morning. We asked a guy what that building was, and I guess we got lucky, because he understood English. He told us that the upstairs floors were an art gallery. After researching this in my "Walking Paris" book when I got back to our room, I discovered that the area was called Les Halles and the multi-hued building was actually the Centre Pompidou, which housed the *Musee National D'Art Moderene,* the National Museum of Modern Art. The museum was actually on Levels 4 and 5 of the edifice and it showcases the history of art from 1960 to the present. So, if you ever get tired of looking at those centuries-old sculptures and paintings of the masters that are on display at the Louvre and other museums, I guess this is the place to come.

Saturday, June 10th

But looking to the left, Carol spotted something that was even more exciting... to her – a mall!! This turned out to be the Forum des Halles, and it was unique in that you had to go down, and then down again to get to the main level of the mall. Since we didn't have any luggage, Carol picked up a couple of necessary items, plus of course, she had to squeeze in a little clothes shopping at the H&M she located in the mall!

After leaving the Forum, we strolled through the piazza and briefly sat amongst the dozens of other loungers who were just sitting outside, chilling. Many of them had brought their blankets to sit on, and quite a few of them had picnic baskets with goodies, and I saw lots and lots of bottles of wine. A perfect place to chill. We sat on the ground for a while before heading back down our street toward the hotel. I'm guessing it was probably only about a mile, or so, from the piazza to the hotel. It probably took us about 25 minutes, or so, of leisurely strolling till we reached the hotel, but then we just kept on walking in the other direction to see what awaited us there. About two short blocks past our hotel, we hit one of the main streets, a grand boulevard in that part of town. As a matter of fact, that was the corner on which our "home" Metro stop was located, and the stop was actually called Grands Boulevards. Looking up and down the boulevard, you could tell that this was an area where a lot of action was. We had passed about four clubs in just the two short blocks between our hotel and this corner; and some of them already had lines forming outside the door, with young people with drinks or cigarettes in their hands, chatting away while they waited to get in, as the sounds of jazz music and the smell of food and more cigarettes filled the air. The corner itself had big restaurants on three of the four corners, with each one having dozens of the little round café tables with two chairs, with all of the chairs facing the street. This was our first hint that people-watching from these vantage points was one of the main past-times in Paris, for both locals and tourists. It did not take us very long to get into this past-time ourselves.

    We saw a couple of empty chairs at a table next to a couple, and I asked the young lady if the seats were taken. Surprisingly, she answered in a distinctly American, East Coast dialect, and said the chairs were all ours. We thanked them and got settled in and ordered. After we had consumed most of our dinner, we struck up a conversation with them and found out that they were Phil and Chelsea from New York. I guess it must have been around 9:30 or 10pm by this time. We did not realize it was so late because the sun was still beaming, and we found out that it did not really set over there this time of year till around 10 or 10:30. Wow! So, we engaged in conversation, including US politics, of course, and had a few rounds of drinks; and before you knew it, I looked at my watch and it was 2:30am. All of a sudden, our first day in Paris had become a very long one. But I guess the combination of the adrenaline and excitement and good conversation and late sunset had kept us going way past the point when we should have crashed. So, we got up, said our goodbyes and wished them Safe Travels, and headed back to the room, where we crashed like two sacks of bricks, in short order.

SUNDAY, JUNE 11TH

Montmartre

On Sunday morning, we awakened to a beautiful day. I pulled back the drapes and opened the shutters, and the bright sunshine joyously streamed into the room. It was about 10 o'clock, and the temperature was well on its way to the forecasted mid-80's. As it turned out, we were very lucky in that we had pretty much perfect weather during our entire trip. The daytime highs ranged from the upper 70's to the low 80's and in the evenings, it usually wound up around 60 degrees or so. There was no rain or threat of rain all the while we were there, just plenty of gorgeous sunshine.

    I quickly got dressed and went downstairs in time to catch breakfast and, so I could bring some back upstairs to Carol. They had a surprisingly nice spread, which would be available to us every morning. Everything was set up on a little table and you had to serve yourself buffet style. There was ham and scrambled eggs, choices of yogurt, fresh fruit cocktail (my favorite), Nutella, bread baskets, crackers, marmalade, and cereal, and orange juice, coffee, or tea. This was more than your typical continental breakfast that one usually gets in small hotels!

It took me a couple of trips to take Carol's breakfast upstairs, as I wanted to make sure she got a full variety. She was still in the shower when I came up the 2nd time, but quickly finished up so she could get her eggs and tea while they were still hot, or at least warm.

We were getting a bit antsy now, as we still had no luggage. When I initially went downstairs for breakfast, I had checked at the front desk to see if our bags had arrived from the airport, and they had not. It was now about five minutes before noon, and we had been told we would receive our bags this morning.

We reluctantly finished dressing and headed for the door with this cloud hanging over our heads. But just about that time, we heard sounds coming from the hallway and there was a knock on the door. We opened the door to see the smiling chambermaid's face, and more importantly, our beautiful luggage, and voila, all was well again! Hallelujah!!! So, we quickly changed into some fresh clothes, and left for our destination for the day – Montmartre.

Montmartre and Sacre-Coeur

I was excited about our journey to Montmartre for a number of reasons. First of all, it would be our first chance to travel Paris's Metro train system together. The Metro is fabulous, and I knew that riding on it and traversing Paris via it again, after 20 years, would be just like riding a bike. It is really so easy to learn and navigate that you can easily re-learn how to use it, just by stepping back into the stations

Sunday, June 11th

and getting on board. We had purchased a "Paris Pass" before we left the states. The 6-day version that we bought gave us unlimited rides on all Paris Metros and buses and even the Funicular ride that took you up the hill over at Sacre Coeur. This was definitely the way to go if you are going to be doing a lot of train-hopping around Paris during your trip. Add to this, that the Paris Pass allows you access into over 60 museums and attractions and allows you to "cut the line" at some, and this pass really pays for itself in relatively short time, if you take advantage of it.

The 2nd and main reason that I was so excited about our trip to Montmartre was that this was where I was going to get one of those street artists to do a drawing/sketch of me. I had one of these done on my first trip to Paris in 1977 and I also had one done on my 2nd trip there in 1997. So now, here it was, 20 years later, and I knew that I had to have one done again. That was really all I wanted out of the trip – a decent rendering of me some 40 years after the 1st one. After that, as far as I was concerned, we could have then packed up and returned to the States… Not! But this was definitely one of the moments I was looking forward to.

There were about 12 main Metro lines (numbered 1 through 12, minus the #5, and including the C) that served all of the Central Paris area that we would be exploring, plus Versailles. These lines interconnected at various stations, so once you knew where you were going, all you had to do was to look on one of the Metro route maps to see which line you would be starting at, and which line(s), if any, you would need to switch to in order to reach your destination. You would just have to trace the line and look at the name of the end-point station in the direction you wanted to go, and make sure to follow the signs in the Metro station to board that train, instead of the one for that particular line that went in the other direction. It may sound a bit complex, but I promise, after you had boarded a couple of trains and gone to a couple of places, you would have the gist of it pretty much down pat. And these trains ran frequently and were very punctual. Other than on our trip out to Versailles, where we had to wait 22 minutes to catch the C train, we never had to wait over about 4 minutes for a train at any other time! If we had this kind of system and efficiency in the Dallas-Fort Worth area where I live, or in any or all other major cities in the United States, cars would be unnecessary.

Our "home" Metro station was *Grands Boulevards* on the #8 line. I found out by checking my Metro map (and by verifying with the Front Desk clerk at our hotel, since this was our 1st time on the Metro) that we would need to get on the #8 and go in direction *Balard* to get to the switching station at *Madeleine*, which was only 3 stations away At *Madeleine*, we would switch to the #12 line and go in direction *Aubervilliers,* to the *Abbesses* station. That would be a slightly longer ride, being about 5 stations away. But as I said before, all of these trains ran quite frequently, on time, and moved pretty swiftly from station to station. So, other than our trip out to Versailles toward the end of our stay, I don't think that any one-way Metro we took, ever took over maybe 15 minutes tops.

As we de-trained and followed the Sortie (exit) signs that would lead us out, I started getting more and more excited. Soon I would be posing in front of a carefully selected Street Artist to get my latest portrait drawn, to immortalize me (for the third time) here in Montmartre!

We entered a winding staircase to start our ascent to street level, and immediately noticed two things. First, the walls had been turned into a canvas, with many Parisian scenes, some of which we would recognize on our way back down, as being from here in the Montmartere area. The 2nd, and most striking, thing was how steep the stairs were. As we circled and circled on our way to the top, you could almost immediately feel the burn! After passing two or three landings, we started to wonder, when would it ever end! At that point, I started counting steps, and was over 200 by the time we reached the top. On the return trip, I started counting at the top, and there were over 300 steps to get to the bottom. I did some research when we returned home and found that this Metro station was actually the deepest one in Paris, going 36 meters, or about 118 feet below ground. If you figure 10 feet per story in a building, that's the equivalent of about a 12-story building! No WONDER we felt the burn and were exhausted when we finally reached the top. We found out later that there are elevators inside that can be taken to the top for those who cannot make the climb, but we did not see them. Upon returning home and reading up about this, we found that they were out of service until September of 2017, so we would not have been able to use them anyway.

I also found out from later research that the *Abbesses* station was opened in 1912 and was known for having one of only two original glass-covered Guimard entrances, called *édicules* (kiosks), left in the Paris Metro system. So, the entrance, itself, is a work of art. It is shown below, along with some of the artwork that lines the walls.

Shortly after exiting the station and walking a few yards, we looked up, and there it was, up on a hill overlooking the entire area – Sacre-Coeur, or to give its entire name, the Basilica du Sacre-Coeur de Montmartre (Basilica of the Sacred Heart). Sacre-Coeur is one of the most impressive edifices in Paris, and one that stuck in my memory over the years. Seems like, whenever I spoke to someone about Paris, I would always wind up mentioning that "Big white church up on the hill" in the artsy district.

Sacre-Coeur actually sits on butte Montmartre, which is the highest point in the city, and it is the 2nd most visited church in Paris, behind the Notre Dame Cathedral. Groundbreaking on this huge travertine building began in 1875 and it was completed in 1914. It is also the 2nd highest point in Paris, behind only the Eiffel Tower, as it sits 130 meters atop Montmartre hill, with its dome rising another 83 meters, for a total of 213 meters. The Eiffel Tower is 324 meters tall.

As we approached the base of the hill and started walking toward the church, the closer it got, the more it loomed over us and became even more impressive. We quickly realized a couple of things. First, there were a whole lot of steps that we would have to traverse just to get to the hilltop level where the base of the church actually started. And next, after only a few steps upward, we got an idea of how steep this climb was going to be. It was much steeper than it looked when first viewed from the city streets, which were already a good distance below us. It was at about this time that I strategically started scoping out a couple of landings that I saw above and beyond, as pit-stops to stop and take a break at, on our way up!

We reached the last landing before reaching the summit after a couple of rest stops, and after maybe fifteen minutes or so had elapsed. Only 50 more steps to go!

After making those last 50 or so steps, we finally reached street level. But there were still a few more steps to go to get to the actual entrance of the church (groan). At this point, Carol turned around and snapped the photo below, which was our first glimpse of Paris from the heights. It gave us a magnificent view over Central Paris looking from the north to the south, and our first glimpse of how tightly all the buildings were packed in, in the city.

*Sunday, June 11*th

It was said that the view from the top of the dome was even better. But at that point, neither one of us felt like climbing the 322 steps inside the church to get to the dome. So, we would just have to be satisfied with this aerial view, for now.

After we took in the sights of Paris, including the Eiffel Tower, and got all the pics we wanted from that vantage point, we decided to head on over to the part of Montmartre where the street artists hung out. My twenty-year-old memory told me that this was back down at the bottom of the hill in town where all the shops were that we had passed on our way up to Sacre-Coeur. At this point, we did not feel like walking all the way back down, so we decided to take the Funicular. The funicular was basically a cable-car that took you on the quick two or three-minute ride back down the hill. One good part about this ride was that it was covered under our Paris Pass, so we did not have to buy additional ride tickets.

We arrived at the bottom of the hill, and with all of those little shops in front of her, Carol decided to do a little shopping. We found a nice little perfume shop, and that's where she actually wound up buying all the bottles of perfume that she would be taking back home as gifts for special family and friends. We walked over one street to where I thought the artists would be, and upon not finding them, I decided to ask one of the retailers who was standing in front of his shop if he knew where the street artists hung out. He told us they were back up the hill on the side street to the left of Sacre-Coeur. So much for my twenty-year-old memory! We got back on the Funicular and took the ride back up to the top, where we had boarded it. Sure enough, a few yards in front and to the left of us, we saw the street that led to the artist's square.

After walking over one block, we came upon the square. It was like going back in time. The square was actually surrounded by cobblestone streets, with restaurants and shops all around the perimeter. About one half of the interior of the square was lined with two or three rows of the street artists. As we walked up and down the rows, we could see that they were at various stages of drawing their subjects, who were posing diligently in front of them. There must have been around twenty or so artists. As we slowly made our way up and down the rows, we took notice of which artist's work looked most like his subject. After two passes, I settled on an artist who was just finishing up his drawing of a young teen-age girl. It was spot-on! A lot of the passers-by agreed, and that settled it for me. This was my guy!

So, after the young girl's parents paid him for her painting, I asked him how much it would be, and since the price he gave was within the budgeted amount in my head, I agreed, and he guided me to the chair and positioned me where he wanted, and we got started.

About 20 minutes or so into the drawing, I was getting a little nervous, because Carol was giving me the thumbs down, meaning it did not really look like me. But all I could do was just sit there, and hope that the further along he got, the more it would look like me. At around the half-hour mark, some of the passers-by started giving me the thumbs-up and/or smiles indicating that he had captured my likeness, so I started feeling a little better. Carol also gave me a thumbs-up at around this same time. Whew!

The artist had told me to take a break and stretch my neck or so, if I ever got tired; but I was doing okay, so I only briefly got out of pose for a few seconds after about 30 minutes. I did not want to move too much, as I did not want to risk changing position. He told me I was a good poser.

At a little over the one-hour mark, he indicated that we were finishing up, and motioned for me to come around and take a peek. A few more folks had passed by and given me good signs by this time, so I anxiously went around the easel and took my first look, with hopeful anticipation. Bingo! He nailed it! I gave him a big hug and a smile, and he finished the painting by signing his name – Aman – in the lower right-hand corner.

I was now immortalized for eternity! As far as I was concerned, we could return to the States right now, as this was the main thing I wanted out of this trip!

So, armed with my new treasure and our growling stomachs, we proceeded to find a restaurant on the piazza to sate our hunger and our appetite for more people-watching.

It didn't take long to find a suitable place to dine. After making one turn on the square and walking back toward Sacre-Coeur, we came across a huge restaurant that actually was on both sides of the street. They had a huge outdoor dining facility on the inside of the square, that had a bunch of large tents that you could dine under – kind of like the ones you might see at Oktoberfest in Munich. And across the street from that, on the side lined with traditional brick and mortar restaurants, they had their main facility. That was the side we chose, primarily because of its people-watching vantage point. This was Au Cadet de Gascogne (4 Place du Tertre, 75018).

*Sunday, June 11*th

Carol and I quickly ordered as we were both famished from all the walking we had done so far. And posing for an hour works up an appetite, as well. Carol settled on the Pennes Bolognaise, which was a beef, onion and carrot laced Penne Pasta, and I went for the Magret de Canard – seared duck breast, with a honey and orange sauce. Excellent choices! Carol washed hers down with a glass of Verre Sancerre white wine, while I chose a French beer, Kronenbourg 1664, to accompany my meal. After an hour or so of languishing over another drink or two, and taking in the pedestrian sights, we finally left Au Cadet. It was around 7:30pm by this time, and we were ready to take it on in, so we strolled on over to the Funicular and caught it back down the hill. After a short walk back to the Metro station, we descended the 300+ steps into the train cavern, and within 30 minutes or so, we were back in our room. It had been a long day, and we had to catch an early train to be over near the Arc de Triomphe by 10am the next day for the start of our Black Paris Walking Tour, so we crashed pretty much hard and heavy as soon as we got back to the room.

MONDAY, JUNE 12TH

Black Paris Walking Tour

This day promised to reveal parts of Paris that the average tourist or visitor would never see. Today was the day of our "Black Paris Walking Tour (BPWT)."

I had booked this tour before leaving, after talking to a friend who mentioned that such things existed. I had then Googled "Black Paris Walking Tour" and found a couple of them. After reading about them, I went with the one that had been formed by Ricki Stevenson, an ex-pat from the Oakland area, who had started her tours back in 1993. After reading up on all that was offered, it seemed that this would, indeed, be a great opportunity to see Paris by looking at a historical context of some of the Black folks - both native French, and some Black Americans - who had lived and worked in France. Finding out that she had received Trip Advisor's "Award for Excellence" and appeared on the Steve Harvey Radio Show in 2013 sort of sealed the deal.

Within hours of having booked the tour online, I received an 8-page PDF Welcome packet from Ricki. It included a lot of information that I did not know about, or had not thought about, including the following:

1. Info on contacting the Paris Super Shuttle to arrange round-trip transportation from the airport to the hotel, and back. I did this.
2. Included the Black Paris Tour Guide to Restaurants, which I used to make dinner plans for 3 or 4 evenings while we were there. This guide had personalized info, like the name of the owner at one restaurant, so we could ask for her and tell her we were guests of BPWT to get special treatment.
3. Included the Black Paris Tour Guide to Jazz Clubs, which I also used.
4. Reminder to call your bank and credit card companies to let them know you would be overseas, so they would not mark your cards as possibly fraudulent, and freeze them while you were there. I may or may not have remembered to do this, but the reminder was nice.

There were many more useful tips covering a myriad of topics. So, as far as I was concerned, booking this tour started paying dividends even before we left the States.

We had to catch our #8 train to the #1 line to get off at the exit by the Arc de Triomphe for our 10am orientation meeting. This was about a 20 or 30-minute ride in total. We met at a restaurant called Café Lateral. Since we arrived around 30 minutes prior to the start of orientation, this gave us our first chance to get a look at the Arc up close and personal.

Our tour group consisted of Carol and me, two other couples, and our guide, Miguel. The older couple was from the Bay Area in California, and the younger one was from the Chicago area.

Miguel was just a wealth of historical information about Paris. One of the things he got into right away was explaining how mostly all the buildings in Paris seemed to look alike – 5-story block-long buildings – no matter what neighborhood or part of Paris you were in. Emperor Napoleon III had commissioned an architect, Georges Haussmann, to redesign some of the major streets and boulevards in the mid 1800's. The first boulevard he designed, rue di Rivoli, served as the model for all the others. The most famous and recognizable feature of Haussmann's renovation of Paris were the Haussmann apartment buildings, which line the boulevards of Paris. Street blocks were designed as homogeneous architectural wholes. He treated buildings, not as independent structures, but as pieces of a unified urban landscape. The Haussmann façade was organized around horizontal lines that often continued from one building to the next. Before Haussmann, most buildings in Paris were made of brick or wood and covered with plaster. Haussmann required that the buildings along the new boulevards be either built or faced with cut stone, usually a cream-colored Lutetian limestone, a local product, which gave more harmony to the appearance of the boulevards.

I am including a picture here of these buildings below. Anyone who has been to Paris will recognize them as the buildings you see all over Paris, for sure.

After Miguel told us about the history of the Haussmann buildings, he got into telling us about some of the Black Americans who had come over to France and made names for themselves in various ways. We learned of Eugene Bullard, who was the first African-American combat pilot ever, flying for France during World War I. He was known as the Black Swallow of Death and the movie

Flyboys, in 2006, was based on the aerial adventures of him and his squadron.

He also told us about James Reese Europe, a Black American ragtime and jazz bandleader, who also distinguished himself in the French military during WWI. He saw combat as a lieutenant with the 369th Infantry Regiment, aka the Harlem Hellfighters and he also led the military band as they travelled over 2000 miles throughout France, entertaining French, British, and American troops and French civilians.

Two of the more famous Black people we learned about who greatly contributed to France's culture were Alexander Dumas and Josephine Baker. As our tour got underway, and we left the restaurant, we got on a bus and traveled to one of our first stops, the park where they had a statue commemorating Dumas. But before I talk about that, I have to talk about bus etiquette. As we boarded the bus, Miguel directed us to the back of the bus. This was not a throwback to 1950's U.S.A., where Blacks had to ride at the back. He explained to us that the middle, wider sections were most commonly reserved for use by the elderly and/or folks with wheelchairs or walkers or mothers with strollers, and the front sections were for the elderly, so they would not have to walk so far to get to the back. This made sense. He also explained that it was common courtesy and expected that if you were seated, and an elderly person got on board, you were expected to offer your seat. They might not take it, but the offer was definitely expected. Paris Bus Etiquette 101!!

We arrived at the park where they had Alexandre Dumas's statue, after a 15-minute or so bus ride. Dumas was most famously known for two of his books, "The Three

Musketeers" and "The Count of Monte Cristo." One of the Musketeers, D'Artagnan, was also sculpted on the base of the statue.

Miguel was obviously passionate about history. I believe that he said that he even got his Master's Degree in History while he was living in Spain. He definitely has found his calling, in making history come alive for folks.

Of all the folks he told us about, the most memorable, and probably the most beloved in France, was Josephine Baker. This native of St. Louis, Missouri left the United States for Paris in 1925 at the age of 19 and never looked back. She instantly became a star in Paris, known for her erotic dancing, and famous for her "banana costume." But she was more than just an entertainer, and she loved her adopted country. She proved it during World War II by serving in the French Resistance against Hitler and Germany, and later did some spy work. After the war, she continued fighting against racism until her death in 1975. On this tour, we were able to go inside the church, from which they had given her a state funeral, L' Eglise de la Madelaine. This church had been started in 1806, after being commissioned by Napoleon, and was completed in 1828. It is a massive Neo-classical building, built in the Roman temple style. Looking at it from the front, it looks like the front view of the Jefferson Memorial in Washington DC.

Getting back to the funeral, Josephine Baker remains the only American-born woman to have received full French military honors. Among the dignitaries attending her funeral were Princess Grace of Monaco and Sophia Loren.

This was a 6-hour tour, and we wound up that afternoon going to a part of Paris called "Little Africa" which was up in the Montmartre part of town. We dined at a Senegalese Restaurant, *(Les Delices du Sacre Coeur, 52 rue de Clingnancourt)* and got to sample some West African cuisine, including things like Chicken Yassa (from Mali), Beef Maffe (beef in peanut sauce), Theibou Djene (rice, vegetables and fish from Senegal), and Aloko (sweet fried plantains from West Africa). All of this was washed down by ginger punch and bissap (made from Hibiscus leaves, much like the sorrel that My Jamaican wife Carol makes during the holidays).

After leaving the restaurant, our final destination was a walk up and down a couple of the streets of Little Africa. It was very colorful, and we got to see some of the wares that the African vendors and store owners had brought from their countries to Paris. One thing that stood out was that it seemed as though about half the stores sold African fabric that you could buy and make your own clothes out of. We then ran across the store of an African gentleman, who was a tailor and clothing designer, who had designed all of the clothes in the store. They were a bit too colorful and loud for my tastes, but this gentleman was a character, so I have to show him here. He reminded me of a Black Leprechaun and his name was Mr. Bachelor.

Monday, June 12th

TUESDAY, JUNE 13ᵀᴴ

Notre-Dame and Seine River Cruise

We got up and went downstairs relatively early on Tuesday morning to catch breakfast. A Buffet Breakfast was made available every morning until 10:30, and we wanted to have a full belly that morning before heading out. Breakfast was included as part of our package, and when you are booking your hotel or package in Paris, you may want to make sure that you get a deal where it is included. I checked with our hotel, and if it had NOT been included, that would have been about $11 USD per day per person, or roughly $150 extra for a one-week stay. They had a full complement to choose from – ham and eggs, cereal, fruits, breads and jams, tea, orange juice, and coffee, but that still would have been a hefty line item on our bill, had it not been included. Alrighty then… off to Notre Dame.

After getting off the #4 train at the Cite Metro station, we had to walk a couple of blocks to get to Notre-Dame. The first view of it, as you looked across the square that was in front of it, was very impressive. Those two towers were

Tuesday, June 13th

instantly recognizable, after having seen them in numerous movies, TV shows, and advertisements for Paris through the years.

This was a grand and very old structure. Groundbreaking occurred in 1163 and the edifice was completed almost two centuries later, in 1345.

Before getting in the line to go up to the towers, we decided to check out the inside of the church. It was very ornate, with many, many stained-glass windows and a lot of statues of famous Catholic Saints and other persona.

As I said, after finishing our tour of the inside of the cathedral, we had to get in line because, unfortunately, Notre-Dame was one of the places where the Paris Pass did not allow you to bypass the line. And a hefty line it was. It stretched around the side of the church along a side street and it took us about an hour to get in. During the course of our journey from the back of the line to the front, I had my first Crepe in Paris. One of our friends had given us rave reviews about the crepes in Paris, so I was really looking forward to that. The one I had, with cinnamon and bananas, was okay, but did not live up to the hype.

Upon finally reaching the front of the line, we found that they were letting folks in, in about groups of twenty or so, to start that trek up to the Towers. We had to wait in a little fenced off area until the group in front of us had cleared. Once it was our turn, I saw why only a limited amount of folks could go up at a time. Almost immediately upon entry, you entered a narrow, winding staircase. It was barely wide enough for two people, and it was very steep. After about maybe 75 or 80 steps, and two or three "landings" or rest-stops, I was already winded and had to let some young folks behind us pass. After another couple of dozen steps, or so, we finally entered a room that looked like a gift shop, with some little pamphlets about the church and a couple of Cathedral officials. But this was actually another staging area, where they kept you until the group in front cleared. I guess we were there for maybe five or ten minutes before we were allowed to start going up some more. The steps were still just as steep, and the passage had even gotten a little narrower. After maybe another 100 steps, or so, we finally arrived at the first viewing level in the tower. This was the level where all the Gargoyles were, and

Tuesday, June 13th

it was magnificent! I had always loved the gargoyles and I still have a replica of Quasimodo, the Hunchback of Notre-Dame, in my office back home, so this was very special for me. As we started moving around the landing, the gargoyles were everywhere. They were so close that you could actually reach through some of the mesh fences and touch some of them.

And the views of Paris were amazing from this level. To the west, you could see the Eiffel Tower and to the north, there was Sacre-Coeur.

The Seine River was right below us with the Seine River cruise boats viewed, going in both directions. You could clearly see where the Seine forked from this vantage point, as well. And we were not even all the way up to the top of the tower yet!

After spending around 20 or 30 minutes viewing Paris from every angle of the tower at this level, it was time to hit the staircase again for that final ascent to the top. Carol decided that she had gone high enough at this point, and she chose to go back down instead. So, we said our goodbyes, and after much huffing and puffing and another 10 minutes

Tuesday, June 13th

or so (it seemed like an eternity!), I finally emerged on the top level. The views from up here seemed even more far-reaching. Perhaps it was because there were not any mesh fences or netting encumbering the views. There were just buildings packed in upon buildings in every direction. Of course, you could still view all of the same major monuments as below, but from up here we also saw a thick cloud of black smoke emerging from some buildings off to the southwest. No one was able to identify exactly what structures were on fire (we were all tourists, for goodness sake), but something was definitely amiss. After a few seconds of gawking at the smoke, we continued our walk around the tower. This was definitely the highest vantage point that we had been on, since we arrived. We were some 422 steps (226 feet) above ground level, according to the brochures, and trust me, my calves and lungs reflected the toll that each step had effected on them. But I can honestly say that it was definitely worth it.

And so, now, the downward journey began. Although it was obviously easier going down, it was still no stroll through the park, and I still needed to take numerous rest stops on the way down. I had started counting steps at the top, and when we reached the bottom, I was at 395. I don't know what happened to those other 27 steps, but maybe it was because we were led down a different route. Carol was waiting for me at ground level in that initial waiting area, so I reconnected with her and we said our goodbyes to Notre Dame.

It was around mid-afternoon when we finished with Notre-Dame, and we had definitely walked up an appetite. There was a restaurant right on the corner directly across the street from the cathedral, and we decided that was as good a place as any. So, we found an empty table in front of the café and settled in for a little time of dining and people-watching. We quickly noticed a heavy military presence in the area. There were many groups of soldiers walking around, eyes ever darting to and fro. They mostly traveled in groups of four, and some of them had their fingers on the triggers of their automatic rifles, ready to fire at a moment's notice. It is important to note here that Paris had had about four major terrorist incidents/attacks around various tourist attractions and monuments just in the first five months of this year, so the military presence was no joke. They wanted to make sure they had a visible presence.

Obviously, they did not want any pictures taken of them either. Some folks at the table next to ours must have had their camera pointed in the soldier's direction when they took some pics, because straightaway one of them came over to their table and asked them what they had been taking pictures of. They made them show them their most recent photos and then they made them delete them. They were not playing around!

Seine River Cruise

After a couple of hours of dining and people-watching, we headed back to the Metro station to catch the train. We actually walked over to the St. Michel, a different station than the one we arrived at, so that we would not have to switch lines. This #1 train would take us down to the Champ de Mars station by the Eiffel Tower – only four stops away - from which it would be only a short walk down the street to the pier where we would board our river cruise boat.

After exiting the Champ de Mars station and going up to ground level, we spotted the Eiffel Tower, two or three

Tuesday, June 13th

blocks away and started walking toward it, since our boarding location for the cruise, Pier 3, was supposed to be opposite the tower. As we walked down the street, Carol asked a woman who was speaking English if she knew where the cruise boats were, and sure enough, she said we were heading in the right direction. One thing I noticed that was prevalent all along the path from the Metro to the Tower was guys, who were set up playing the "Shell Game" to see if they could lure any unsuspecting tourists into their trap. One of the guys even asked me if I was interested, after showing us, with one of their confederates playing the role of a tourist (of course, we were not supposed to figure that out), how easy it was. I politely declined.

After walking a few minutes, the Eiffel Tower suddenly burst into view on our right. C'est Magnifique! We took a few minutes to take it in, before we headed on toward the pier. We had already booked our Eiffel Tower tour for the next day, so we knew that, soon enough, we would really get up close and personal at that time.

The Seine River cruise was another item that was included with our Paris Pass, so all we had to do was go up to the ticket window and show them our pass to get the tickets, and then basically walk right on board. Even though there was a very short line, the boat was almost completely full when we boarded. It was bigger than it looked, and there must have been at least 200 people or so on board. It took us a few minutes to find seats together, but we finally did.

Our cruise lasted about an hour and it gave us some amazing vantage points, from which to see some of the major monuments in the city. As we left the Eiffel area, traveling from west to east. I believe, the first one we saw on our right was the Musee d' Orsay, and almost directly across the street from it, on the other bank, was the Louvre. This was good info to file away because we were going to visit the Louvre in a couple of days; and now I saw how close Orsay was to it – perhaps just a 10 or 15-minute walk across the Seine.

We kept going, and shortly, we came to a fork in the river, and we took the right fork. I remember having seen where it forked, looking down from Notre-Dame earlier that day, and sure enough, as we looked up and to the left, there was Notre-Dame, in all her glory.

A little further along, to the left, we were able to get a good view of the Luxor Obelisk, which stands in the middle of the Place de la Concorde square. The Obelisk looked just like our Washington Monument in Washington DC, only it was yellow, having been carved from yellow granite. It is about 75 feet high and decorated with hieroglyphs honoring King Ramses II. That made sense, because it originally sat at the entrance of the Luxor Temple in Egypt, until it was gifted to France by Muhammad Ali Pasha, the Ruler of Egypt, in 1833.

As we cruised up the river, we could see people all up and down the Left Bank, on the grass that bordered the river, just chilling. Some of them waved to the boat as we glided past them, and some passengers, including us, waved back. At one point, we saw a young man riding a bike along the bike and pedestrian path, and he must have "popped a wheelie" for a good 20 or 30 seconds, it seems. All in all, it was just a peaceful, idyllic ride, and an excellent way to spend part of a beautiful afternoon in Gay Paree!

WEDNESDAY, JUNE 14ᵀᴴ

Carol's Birthday and The Louvre

Well, this was it. Today was the reason we decided to come over to Paris at this time of year. It was Carol's birthday and we had decided to celebrate it somewhere special. I figured I would get a lot of Brownie points for this one! And it sure beat the box of chocolates or dozen roses, or any of those things that I normally gave her for her birthday.

We hopped on our regular train at the Grands Boulevards Metro station and transferred over to the #1 line at Chatelet – Les Halles. It is worth noting here that the Chatelet – Les Halles Metro station is the largest underground station in the world! Three of the RER suburban lines and five metro lines converge at this interchange station and it is the central node of the Metro network. Up to 750,000 passengers pass through this hub every day, and at peak times, it can see 120 trains in an hour!

Wednesday, June 14th

Our destination exit, Palais Royal Musee du Louvre, was just one exit away from Chatelet. One thing we noticed and reflected on after a couple of days of riding the Metros was that we had never had to wait more than 5 minutes to catch a train to this point, and in fact, we had caught most in 2 minutes or less. These Paris Metros were fast, on-time and efficient! This particular exit connected directly with the Louvre Museum, and as we walked through the station, toward the Museum, there were just droves of people marching in front of, and behind us. It kind of reminded me of when we had been in the Vatican in Rome the previous fall, in the Sistine Chapel. There was that same sense of being in a herd of cattle, just getting pushed along with the flow. But when you were on your way to the largest and third most visited museum in the world, (the other 2 are in China) I guess you can expect no less!

The Louvre

After walking for about five minutes or so, we noticed that it seemed as though, all of a sudden, we had entered a mall, or shopping area of some sort. There were stores on both sides of us, and they all looked very swank. Some of the names that I noticed were Esprit, Swarovski, Le Tanneur, and Fossil, among others. We walked a few hundred yards past these, and all of a sudden, we were in a giant rotunda-looking area with people going every which way. I noticed a restaurant on the upper level, and some escalators off to the right that went upstairs. There were a couple of information desks in close proximity to us, so I stopped at one of them and asked which way we needed to go to get into the museum. They told me that, if we had our tickets already, we just needed to go up the escalator and pass through the security check, and we would be there. We had our Paris Passes, which got us free entry into the Louvre, so up we went, and after only a minute or two in line, and another minute or two going through a pretty cursory security check, we were in!

That was pretty cool getting in that quickly and easily. After we got back home, and I did a little digging, I found out that the underground mall we had entered into directly from the Metro station, was called *Carrousel de Louvre*. In regard to the Louvre, it was sometimes referred to as one of the "secret entrances" that allowed you entry without having to endure the long waits often found at one of the four main entrances. So, just by taking the Metro directly to the Palais Royal Musee du Louvre exit and entering the museum via that route, we had inadvertently apparently cut a significant amount of time from our journey. This was definitely a piece of information that we would file away and use during our next trip to Paris and the Louvre!

It was around High Noon when we actually entered the museum. Naturally, the first thing we wanted to see was the Mona Lisa, so we started looking around for signs that might point us toward her. I saw a sign that pointed us down a long hallway with a wide staircase at the end of it. It said we were supposed to go to the Denon Wing to find Ms. Lisa, so off we headed down the hallway.

As we approached the staircase, (which I later learned was called the *Daru Staircase)* I spotted the first piece of art that was instantly recognizable. It was the *Winged Victory* (full name = Winged Victory of Samothrace). Basically, this was the statue that looked like a headless angel, wings and all!

Wednesday, June 14th

    This giant Parian Marble statue stands about 8 feet tall and was completed in 190 B.C. It is a Hellenistic sculpture representing Nike, the Greek goddess of Victory. (Now we know where that shoe company got its' name from!)

After taking a few pictures of this impressive sculpture, we took a right turn and headed down the hallway, following the signs that said "Mona Lisa." We were on the 1st level of the Denon Wing. After maybe 100 yards or so, if that, we came to a large, open room, and judging by the size and density of the crowd at the far end of this room, there was no doubt that this was where Mona lived! I peeked over some of the shorter folks and got my first glimpse of her, and excitedly pointed her out to Carol!

Wednesday, June 14th

That was the first time I saw her show any real excitement or emotion since we entered the museum. We walked toward the throng, which must have been maybe ten-deep all the way around that half of the room, forming a semi-circle in front of the painting. As I tried to see where I could edge in a little closer, I glanced to my right, and saw that Carol had already made a path for herself and was only about 2-deep away from Mona already! Great job Carol!! She was already in "Selfie" mode, with her back to the painting, taking pictures over her shoulder. After about 5 or 10 minutes of gently elbowing and nudging my way forward, I finally reached the rope that separated the multitudes from greatness. Even though this was my 3rd time seeing Mona Lisa, it still was kind of surreal, seeing what is generally considered to be one of the greatest paintings of all time. If not the greatest, it is assuredly the most famous. Da Vinci did good. *(Interesting Note: This painting, which was started on in 1503 and believed to have been completed in about 1517, is thought to be one in which the subject was Lisa Gherardini, wife of Francesco Giocondo)*

After getting our fill of pictures, we snaked our way back through the crowd to the middle of this very large room. The last time I had seen Mona Lisa, in 1997, I'm sure she was on a side wall, and not nearly as isolated by herself as she was now, at the end of this huge room. I guess maybe the demand to see her has gone up over the years… or something.

The Louvre is very large, and not that easy to navigate through. Unless you have an exact idea of what you want to see and where it is, you can easily spend hours just kind of aimlessly wandering or getting caught up in some of the artwork. I know the last time that I was there, in 1997, I actually spent about four hours or so just looking at and studying ONE painting. The painting kind of told a story as you progressed through it from left to right. I was on the lookout for that painting again during this visit, but I don't believe I saw it.

I only had one more piece of art that I wanted to really see before we left, and Carol didn't have any. I wanted to find that famous sculpture with both arms broken off, Venus de Milo. From our map, we saw that she was down on Level 0 in the Sully Wing, and we were currently on Level 1 in Denon. So, we decided to just play it by ear a bit and keep going down this wing until we reached the end of it to see what we would run into.

The first thing we saw that was kind of interesting was a young female artist who actually had her easel set up and was painting a copy of one of the original paintings that hung on the wall. As you can see from my photo below, she did a remarkable job of capturing the original.

Wednesday, June 14th

Who knew that this kind of thing happened? I certainly didn't. But upon Googling the topic while writing this section of this book, I found that it was quite a common occurrence at various museums around the world, and especially, apparently, at The Louvre. I had just never seen any artists in action copying the "masters" on any of my previous visits to the museum.

The only other painting I saw of interest on this level was a huge painting of what looked like one humdinger of a feast! There were people pouring out wine from big urns, and folks playing cellos and other instruments, and just a general sense of everyone having a marvelous time. The really curious thing about this painting was that, right smack in the middle of it, seated in the middle of a table like the one in The Last Supper painting, there sat Jesus, halo and all! He was looking directly OUT of the painting, right at the viewer, while everyone else in the painting was engaged with other people. When I researched this painting, I found that it was entitled *The Wedding at Cana* and was painted by Paolo Veronese in 1563. Apparently, it is the depiction of an actual story from The Bible, in which Jesus turns water to wine (John 2: 1 -11). This was the story where Jesus, His mother Mary, and some of the apostles attended a wedding feast in Cana, and when the wine ran out, Mary asked Jesus to turn some water into wine, which he did. So that explains the wine jugs in the painting. It really is amazing how much more interesting these paintings become if you learn the back stories behind their origin.

We left this level and went down to Level 0, where the first section we came to was the Arts of Africa, Asia, Oceania and the Americas. There works consisted mostly of sculptures, and I guess my African roots must have come out, because I found most of the African sculptures very interesting. The first one that I am showing below is one of a sphinx, The Great Sphinx of Tanis.

This is the first thing you see when you enter the Egyptian collection section. This is one of the largest sphinxes outside of Egypt. It weighs about 26 tons! It was found in 1825 among the ruins of the Temple of Amun at Tanis (the capital of Egypt during the 21st and 22nd dynasties). **According to archaeologists, certain details**

Wednesday, June 14th

suggest that this sphinx dates to an earlier period - the Old Kingdom (c. 2600 BC). Some people believe that this sphinx is the guardian of the Egyptian collection in the museum and even of the Louvre itself.

Here are two more sculptures from the African section that I found interesting.

As I may or may not have mentioned, The Louvre is HUGE! By this time, we had probably been in the museum for maybe an hour-and-a-half or so and I was basically just ready to go find the Venus de Milo statue and call it a wrap. I believe that Carol felt the same way. It can get overwhelming as you pass through the halls and just see more and more paintings and sculptures. So, we were definitely ready to boogie.

I don't know if I actually planned it, or whether we got lucky, but as we kept walking down the main hallway on the floor we were on, past the Roman Antiquities and the Italic and Etruscan Antiquities, we came to the end of that hallway, and Boom – there she was… Ms. De Milo, in the flesh… er um, I mean in the marble!

With this viewing of the 3rd of the Big Three Ladies of the Louvre – Winged Victory, Mona Lisa, and Venus de Milo, we felt that we had 'done' the Louvre, enough for this trip, and we started heading toward that central area, from which we had spotted a cafeteria earlier. It was around 2pm by this time, and we had definitely walked up an appetite!

We opted for something familiar from the menu, so I simply had a Burger Efiloche (Pulled-pork sandwich), fries, and a Heineken, and Carol had a Burger Poulet (Chicken sandwich), fries and a Peach Tea. It was refreshing, and we quickly finished it because we had one more stop before heading home. This was going to be a full day.

Musee d' Orsay

We exited the Louvre through the Sortie that led to that famous glass Pyramid that stands in the courtyard, and got our bearings to get to the Musee d' Orsay. Orsay is one of the other major museums in Paris, and it is pretty much directly across the Seine River, on the left bank, from The Louvre. It only took us about 15 minutes to get to it. It really only took 5 minutes to reach it, but then it is such a huge building, with the entrance all the way around on the other side, that's why it took 15 minutes to get to the entrance. Orsay does not have any super-duper famous paintings or sculptures that would be easily recognizable, like the Louvre has, but the building itself is a piece of architecture worth seeing. It was originally a train station, built in 1900 for the Exposition Universalle, which was like a World's Fair of its time. It was converted to a museum and opened as such in 1986.

Orsay is definitely easier to navigate than The Louvre. When you first enter and walk into that wide-open

Wednesday, June 14th

space, it definitely still has the feel of a train station, kind of like Grand Central Station in New York. There is a huge clock mounted on the stained-glass windows down at the far end of the hall and that is one of the centerpieces of attraction upon entry.

s I said, Orsay did not have any major works of art, or at least not any that would be recognized by the casual visitor or tourist. But I am including two below that really caught my eye. The first:

This piece is called *Les Quatre Parties du Monde* (The Four Parts of the World) and was sculpted by Jean-Baptiste Carpeaux around 1872 It represents the four parts of the world (Europe, Asia, Africa, and America) supporting the celestial sphere. Pretty cool!

The next piece that I want to show here is actually a collection:

This collection was created by Charles Cordier from 1856 – 1861. From left to right, the pieces are: An Algerian Man, African Woman, and Negro from the Sudan. I found out from my research after returning home that this bust of the African woman is the only depiction of a Black woman in the entire museum. Interesting...

As I mentioned, Orsay was laid out nicely with just two levels to navigate, so we strolled around and enjoyed the art we did see, and before you knew it, we had been in there about 90 minutes. Uh, oh, worked up another little appetite!

As it turned out, we were right next to the dining establishment in this museum, so we popped in there to get a light desert. This dining room itself looked like a mini-museum corridor, what with the paintings on the ceiling a la the Sistine Chapel, and the art deco chairs and tables. Quite an eclectic mix!

We left Musee d' Orsay at around 5:30 pm and caught the Metro back to our hotel so that we could change for one of the major events of the trip – Carol's Birthday Dinner!

CAROL'S BIRTHDAY DINNER

I had started planning on the venue for Carol's Birthday Dinner even before we left the States. After I signed us up for the *Black Paris Tours*, they sent us a brochure that included some of their recommended restaurants and jazz clubs. I found a restaurant called *Autour du Midi Restaurant and Jazz Club* that seemed to fit the bill perfectly for what I wanted for Carol. It was advertised as one of the best of the historic Montmartre jazz venues. I loved the Montmartre area, and it was only about three Metro stops away from us, so this definitely was where I wanted to take her. Ricki Stevenson, the owner of Black Paris Tours, said that I would not have to make reservations until we got to Paris. So, I started calling them a couple of days before Carol's birthday, but kept getting busy signals and an answering machine. I also asked the Front Desk of our hotel to call them for me while we were out during the day, but all they got was the voice-mail as well. I chalked this up to them just being very busy, and I decided that we would just go over there without reservations and take our chance. Besides, at that point, it was too late to make reservations anywhere else that required them, so we were kind of out there.

We got to the Metro exit by the restaurant at about 9pm. I found the street that the restaurant was on, only about a half-block or so away from our Metro stop, so that was good. We walked up the slightly inclined street and could see Sacre Coueur up at the top of the hill at the end of the street. I got to the address and saw the name of the restaurant above the door... but the restaurant was boarded up! Are you kidding me?!! I could not believe this. I had gotten Carol all hyped up for this special evening and she looked so gorgeous. I was Pissed with a Capital P!! But the best laid plans... right? So, I had to switch to Plan B. The Moulin Rouge, that famous cabaret, was only about a block away, so I went and checked with them in regard to dining, but they said the earliest that they could get us in was at 11pm, about 2 hours from now. That would not do. I went back and broke the news to Carol, and we decided to go back to one of the restaurants on the corner right down the street from our hotel. It was called "La Porte Montmartre." It was about 10:15 when we got seated. We chose an outdoor table so that we could at least get some more people watching in. "Maybe we can salvage this evening after all, I thought."

It was a lovely warm evening, probably in the mid-70's. The weird thing to us was that it was after 10pm and it was still as bright as if it were 6pm or so. This still took some getting used to. We ordered a carafe of white wine – *Alsace Edelzwicker* – to calm our nerves and, as the wine and gentle breeze and overall ambience of the setting kicked in, we ordered and enjoyed our dinner. I had the *Duck Confit with Baby Potatoes* and Carol had the *Veal Brawn with Gribiche Sauce*. Both got Two Thumbs up! As we were finishing up, the gent at the next table called over and asked if we had enjoyed our meal. I replied that 'Yes, we had' and before long he and his wife pulled their chairs over to join us.

He turned out to be a native 42-year old Frenchman named Olivier, and his wife was a 50-year old Filipina, who went by Pim, an abbreviation of her given name, Pimara. Olivier offered to buy us an after-dinner mint alcoholic drink, which was very nice, when he found out it was Carol's birthday. As our conversation progressed, we found that these were lovely people, easy to talk to, and very much, down-to-earth – kind of like us (smile)! They both worked in some type of sales capacity at the main Louis Vuitton store over on the Champs-Elysees, and they told us some stories about their encounters with Paris Hilton and Rihanna when they came in to do their shopping. They said that Rihanna was very polite and appreciative of the service given, whereas Paris was very snobby and just walked around pointing to things she wanted as she passed them. They each would purchase tens of thousands (if not hundreds) of Euros worth of merchandise during each visit!

As the clock approached 1am, Olivier ordered a couple of glasses of celebratory champagne for Carol and me. The conversation was still flowing, and the people were still strolling the boulevard, so we kept chatting. Mind you this was a Wednesday night, not a weekend evening. After one final round, and some tips about good restaurants in the area for future dining, Olivier and Pim gave us their business cards, and we regretfully said our goodbyes, and walked the two blocks to our hotel. It was 2:45am when we walked into the hotel lobby.

THURSDAY, JUNE 15TH

*Grevin Wax Museum, Eiffel Tower,
and 'Obama' Restaurant*

On Thursday, our morning got off to an alarming start… literally. We were awakened mid-morning by the sound of the fire alarm going off in our hotel. This was very scary, as the first thing that popped into my mind was the reports we had been seeing over the last couple of days on our TV, about the devastating Grenfell Tower apartment fire in London that had killed 80 people. But Carol beat me up and out and down the stairs, as I still took the time to grab our passports and my wallet.

After walking down the narrow stairway passage from our 3rd floor room, when I reached the lobby, there were only three other people there – the Front Desk clerk - Odeta, Carol, and a guy who looked like an electrician. I say this because he had a bunch of tools and was standing in front of some type of electrical panel. Odeta told us that the alarm had accidentally gone off while the electrician was doing some of his routine work, and there was nothing to be 'alarmed' about – pun intended! So, with that, we hopped on the slow-moving elevator and went back up to our room to get ready for the real adventures that awaited us that day.

The first reservation that we had booked for that day was a Behind-the-Scenes Eiffel Tower Tour at 4:30pm. So, we had plenty of time to have a nice leisurely morning and early afternoon before catching our Metros to the Eiffel Tower. We had actually booked that tour via Viator before we left the States. I definitely recommend this tour. The main reason that I chose it was because our Paris Pass did not include entrance to the Eiffel Tower. This tour not only got us entrance, and a "skip-the-lines" feature, but also had the bonus feature of touring the underground bunker connected to the Eiffel Tower beneath Champ de Mars park, and also would give us a tour of the underground engine room and hydraulic lift machinery that controlled the Tower. So, we were really looking forward to that.

But first up for us was the Grevin Wax Museum. This museum was included with our Paris Pass, and was only a couple of blocks away from our hotel. We had actually passed it a few times on our stroll around our neighborhood. The quality of the wax figures in the museum was pretty good, and most of the figures that we knew or recognized bore a pretty good resemblance to the person they were supposed to be. There were quite a few persons from French history, who we obviously didn't know; but there were also quite a few current modern American and European celebrities, political, or other folks who we DID know or recognize. I'm including a couple of my favorites here: Carol with President Barack Obama and Queen Elizabeth, and me, with two of my favorite jazz and blues musicians – Ray Charles and Louis Armstrong.

We breezed through the Grevin in probably a little over an hour. They had some kind of mandatory 10-minute introductory presentation, which I totally did not get, but once we completed that, you could go through the rest of the museum at your own pace. This was not the most exciting place we had visited on our trip, but it was definitely a nice way to chill and kill a little extra time… especially since it was covered with our Paris Passes!

We left the Grevin around 2:30, with still plenty of time to get over to the Eiffel for our 4:30 tour. We made the short half-block walk to our regular 'home' Metro Station – Grands Boulevards, and took the train to the RER C line Invalides station, five stops away. From there, it was just another two exits and we got off at the Champ de Mars – Tour Eiffel exit, just a couple of blocks away from the Tower.

We had to walk quite aways underground in this station before exiting, and shortly after we got off the train, we ran into a little excitement. As we rounded a short bend in the walkway, three guys came sprinting toward us at breakneck speed. They looked kind of like Africans, but they were running so hard, I thought they might be kin to my wife's countryman, Usain Bolt, of Jamaica! At first, I thought that maybe they were running to catch the train. But a few seconds after they passed us, a group of three cops almost ran us over, as they jetted by - with guns drawn - in obvious pursuit of those guys! Within a few seconds, two more groups of cops blew past us, with four cops in each group. They had on different style uniforms, so who knows, maybe some of them were city police, and some may have been military. They were moving so fast, we did not get a chance to get a really good look at their uniforms. Wow! Wasn't that special??!!! Carol and I just looked at each other, and I could tell that she was as startled… and relieved as I was, that no shots had been fired! In a narrow hallway like that, I can just imagine that bullets would have been flying everywhere and bouncing off the walls, every which way.

I'm sure that's why those officers probably made a conscious decision to NOT fire their weapons in that tunnel. Alright then!!

As we exited into daylight, we were still a little shaken by our close call. I don't know what those guys did, but it must have been something pretty bad, to have three groups of cops in pursuit!

We crossed the street and saw the sign pointing in the direction of the Tower. Even though it was one of the tallest structures in Paris, we could not see it from this vantage point, due to all the other buildings being in the way. So, we walked as directed by the signs, and within a couple of blocks, there it was. Of course, we had seen it earlier in the week when we took our Seine River cruise, and even got pictures of it from the Seine, but this would be our first time actually setting foot on the grounds of the Eiffel Tower. We still had about an hour before meeting our tour guide, so after we found the place where we were supposed to meet her, we strolled around the grounds and got some good shots. Here's one of my favorites:

Thursday, June 15th

After taking some photos from ground level, we still had time to order a couple of foot-long dogs and beer from one of the refreshment stands. These dogs hit the spot... until the mustard hit the back of your throat. I thought it was just regular Dijon Mustard, but it was like Dijon on steroids! It was so strong, it almost took your breath away. Neither one of us could take another bite after the mustard kicked in, and a cold beer never felt as refreshing as that one did then!

By this time, it was about time to meet our guide, so we moseyed on over to the meeting place, which was only about 10 yards or so away from where we had been sitting and eating. At first, we got with the wrong group, but we were directed to the English-speaking guide a few yards to our right. Our guide, Tanya from Russia, quickly rounded up the dozen or so people in our group, and within 5 minutes or so, we were on our way to our first stop – the underground bunkers beneath the tower. We had no idea exactly where these bunkers were, but as Tanya led us through the exit and off the grounds of the Tower, it quickly became apparent that they were not directly beneath the tower, as I had kind of speculated they might be. She led us into the adjacent park, the Champ de Mars, and after maybe 100 yards or so, we came to a little nondescript gate, and she showed the guard her credentials and led us down the stairs. Apparently, this bunker had been used as a communications bunker during World War I, housing equipment, and also serving as an evacuation route, as part of a complex underground network beneath the tower. Very interesting!

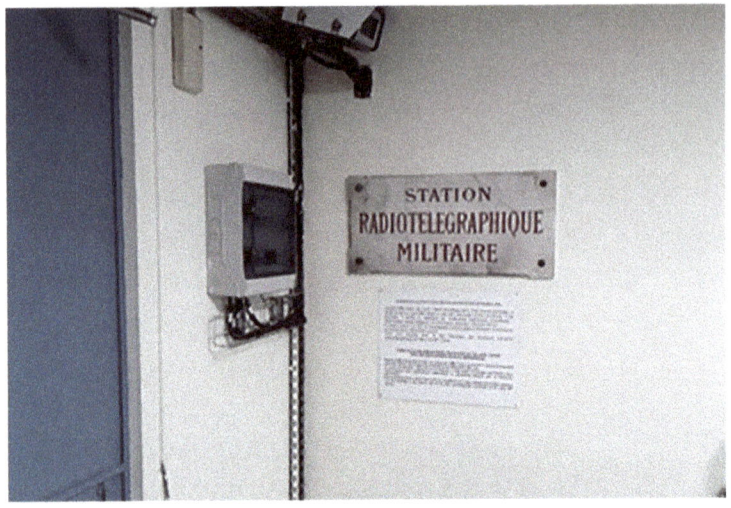

After a few minutes in this area, Tanya led us back up and out and back onto the Tower grounds. We took a short flight of stairs down, and within minutes, we were in the Engine Room, where all the machinery was that powered the huge hydraulic elevators, as well as all the other electrical equipment necessary to operate and illuminate the tower. This was very interesting indeed, and something that the average tourist or Tower visitor would not even think about, let alone visit.

After giving us a little info about some of the equipment we were viewing, Tanya let us wander around for a few minutes, and then we boarded one of the hydraulic elevators and headed for the 2nd level of the Tower. The elevator made a brief stop at ground level, and that's where we normally would have been waiting in line to get on, without the benefit of this tour. I could see the line snaking around for quite a bit on the outside. After our pit stop, we continued on up to the second level. That is where the prestigious *Le Jules Verne* Michelin-starred restaurant resides, along with its private rooftop terrace with the incredible panoramic views of Paris. This tour allowed us access to the terrace, which was normally reserved for Tower employees. We then ended the tour on the 2nd-level balcony. But Tanya told us where and how to purchase tickets to go up to the 3rd level if we wanted to, and then bid us adieu. Since you had to stand in one pretty long line to get tickets, and then in another one to go up to the top, Carol and I decided to just see what we could see from the 2nd level and let that suffice. We were still quite high, and there were definitely some excellent views to be seen from all sides. Here are a couple of them. The first is a selfie that Carol took of us a little closer to the top.

The next one is of me with the Paris "24" logo on that big black tower off in the distance. That stands for the 2024 Olympics, which Paris was in the running to get during the time we were over there. About six weeks after we left, they were awarded the bid.

Thursday, June 15ᵗʰ

We left the Tower at about 7pm and started our journey over to the "Obama" Restaurant for our 8pm dinner reservation. The Eiffel Tower was definitely one of the highlights of our tour, thus far; and that Tour that we purchased to go underground and see the inner workings was the icing on the cake!

As we strolled through Champ de Mars park for the short walk to the restaurant, my wife remarked on how beautiful all the flowers that we were passing looked and smelled. Here were roses and many other varieties of flowers in red and white and yellow and orange and purple hues, and the fragrance was absolutely enchanting, according to Carol! The warm, gentle breeze carried the fragrance all along the path. It smelled just like some of the perfume that Carol had purchased a few days earlier over in Montmartre.

When we got to the first major street that ran through the park, we made a left turn and walked about a block over to the stop-light. I perused the various street signs and saw that the street we wanted was just across the street – a little side street going off at an angle. We entered that street, paved with cobblestone, and after a short walk of maybe two blocks, there it was on our right – the "Obama" Restaurant.

The real name of the "Obama Restaurant" is La Fontaine de Mars. It is located at 129 rue Saint Dominique, 75007. We were initially made aware of this iconic restaurant by the information packet we received after we purchased Ricki Stevenson's Black Paris Tour. It was touted as being the restaurant where President and Michelle Obama chose to dine (instead of having dinner with then French President Sarkozy) during his first visit to France as President back in June of 2009. The Obamas left the girls and Mrs. Robinson at the hotel, and dined on main courses consisting of *Lamb* and *Steak Frites* (Steak and French Fries). *Steak Frites* is apparently a Classic dish in Paris (some high-end restaurants, like Le Relais de l'Entrecote, 20 rue Saint Benoit, 75006) have it as the ONLY menu item), so obviously our classy President and his wife had done their homework!

The package had also told us that when we called to make our reservations after arriving in Paris, that we should ask for the owner, Madame Boudon, and tell them that we were guests of Black Paris Tours, and they would hook us up. We did, and they did!

Thursday, June 15th

When we gave the gentleman at the front door our names, and asked if Madame Boudon was available, he said that she was, and he would go and get her. Within a couple of minutes, he was back and presented us to her and she started fawning over us, making us feel very welcome. She said that friends of Ricki Stevenson and BPT were always most welcome here! She had the head waiter go and prepare a special table for us, after we told her that our preference for dining this evening was indoors. He led us to a cozy red leather booth with the fancy red and white checkered, embroidered tablecloth, and within a very short time we were dining on our lovely meal.

We started with a *Melon Au Jambon* (melon with ham) appetizer and then I had the *Canette* (Roast Duckling Fillet with sauce and wine-poached dates) as my main course, and Carol chose the *Bar Aux Olives* (Rosemary Roast with Olives).

About half-way through our meal, I looked up, and who did I see being escorted to another booth but Tibitha and Willie, one of the other couples that had been with us earlier in the week when we did our Black Paris Walking Tour. Obviously, they had read their info packet and got the tip about this place as well! I got up and gave Tibitha a hug, and we exchanged pleasantries, and agreed to meet afterwards when all of us were through dining. Carol and I then got back into our meal, cleansing our palates with some excellent white wine before topping it off with a shared Crème Brulee.

It was a little after 10pm when we finished dining and got ready to meet our new friends outside the restaurant. But, as I took a minute to go and freshen up before hitting the streets, I turned the corner and looked up at the wall, and this is what I saw:

This is a framed copy of the headline from one of the local newspapers, La Depeche, on the day after the Obamas dined here.

I went back to the table and grabbed my phone and Carol and came back and got this shot. I also informed Tibitha and Willie so that they could snap it as well.

We all then sauntered outside and discussed what our next moves were. We all agreed that we wanted to catch the "Twinkling Lights" on the Eiffel Tower the next time they came on. This happened every evening at 10, 11, and Midnight. We were in excellent shape to catch the 11pm twinkling. So, we headed back toward the Champ de Mars park, and already there were people all over the place, most either just sitting on the grass; or those who were more prepared, were sitting on their blankets. Many of them had bottles of wine. After a few minutes, I understood why. Guys hawking wine were all over the place, shouting out, "Cold Wine" or something like that. I asked one of them how much, and I purchased a bottle along with four plastic cups. Just as we were raising our cups for a toast, the Twinkling began! There was an audible "Ooooo" and "Ahhh" from the throng scattered throughout the park, and then there were a few shouts, whistles, and claps. The overall ambience of the moment was amazing! It was perfect. I was in Paris, sitting in the Champ de Mars in front of a twinkling Eiffel Tower, enjoying a glass of wine on a warm midsummer's night eve with my favorite gal. It just doesn't get much better than that!

FRIDAY, JUNE 16TH

Versailles

Up at 9:30 on a Sleep-in Day. Or at least that's what it *should* have been. The cumulative effect of all that walking that we had done over the last 6 days (not to mention a couple of long 3am nights) had finally caught up with both of us. We did NOT want to let go of that bed. But Versailles awaited! Everyone that we had spoken to since arriving in Paris had told us that this was one place we definitely did not want to miss seeing. So, we sucked it up, went downstairs and had a light breakfast, and headed out the door to catch our train to Versailles.

This was going to be our first time going outside the city limits since we had arrived, and it would also be our first time catching the RER C Line train. The RER was not covered by our Paris Pass, so this would also be the only time during our visit that we actually had to purchase some tickets for the train. I believe that we purchased them at the Invalides station, and from there, it got a little tricky.

When we got to the Champ de Mars – Tour Eiffel station to catch the RER C to Versailles Rive Gauche, somehow, we wound up taking the wrong train. I had a sneaking suspicion that something was wrong when almost immediately after we pulled out of that station, we hooked a right and crossed over The Seine. I knew that we were not supposed to do that, so I told Carol that we needed to get off at the next station, Boulainvilliers, and go back in the direction that we had just come from. We did this, and we got off at Champ de Mars Station again. This time, we found another track and saw, for sure, that the train coming into that one was going Direction Rive Gauche, so we got on and went up to the 2nd level. This train was jam-packed, so that confirmed that we were on the way to Versailles. Once we passed the Javel station, that was the final confirmation that I needed.

Versailles is about 12 miles from the center of Paris, and I would estimate that it took us about 45-50 minutes to get there from the Champ de Mars station. There was no doubt when we arrived, because that Versailles Rive Gauche station was the end of the line!

When we walked outside the station – and it was a huge station – all we had to do was see everyone walking off to the right to know which direction we needed to go to get to Versailles. After about a 10-minute walk, we came to a big clearing and looked to the left, and BAM – there it was!

Friday, June 16*th*

The first impression was pretty amazing. It was a HUGE palace! And this used to be someone's home??!!! OMG!!! Yep, it had been built by King Louis XIII in 1624 as a hunting lodge, but the next king, Louis XIV, expanded it starting in 1661 and turned it into the Royal Palace in 1682, when he moved the royal court out there from Paris. Marie Antoinette, who was the wife of King Louis XVI, and the main Entertainment Coordinator for his Royal Court, had a personal estate on the grounds. Today Chateau Versailles functions primarily as a museum, with over 2300 rooms, and the Gardens.

Versailles is so large and there is so much to see and do there, that one could easily spend a couple of days going through it, if you wanted to experience the vast majority. But we chose to only spend about half-a-day there, and it was still overwhelming. The over-the-top opulence and the grandeur was really beyond words, so I am just going to include an array of photographs here, that hopefully will give you at least some idea of the Essence of Versailles.

The Gardens

Friday, June 16th

The Fountains

Lunch in The Gardens

The King's Bedroom

The room was created by Louis XIV in 1701 and was where he lived until his death on 1 September 1715. In this room the royal rising and going to sleep ceremonies took place.

Above the bed, the allegory of France watching over the sleeping King, in relief by Nicolas Coustou, 1701.

The attic, these paintings are from the collection of Louis XIV and are here back in their original setting. They are: The Four Evangelists and

Cæsar's Denarius by Valentin de Boulogne, and, Agar in the Desert by Giovanni Lanfranco.

Friday, June 16th

I had to include this plaque from Louis XIV's Bedroom because I could not believe that they actually had Royal Rising and Going-to-Sleep ceremonies for the King!

On the grounds, in the Courtyard

This was taken in the famous Hall of Mirrors room, which is the palace's most resplendent room. Each of its 17 arched windows is decorated with 21 mirrors, resulting in a stunning spectacle as light reflected off the 357 mirrors! The ceiling looks just like the ceiling in the famous Sistine Chapel at The Vatican in Rome. The Sistine Chapel was painted by Michelangelo, of course, but I was curious as to who actually painted this ceiling. My research indicated that it was primarily done by Charles Le Brun, who was Louis XIV's court painter, and declared by him to be "the greatest French artist of all time." Le Brun also has works hanging in The Louvre and at the Metropolitan Museum of Art in New York City.

As I said, we only spent about 3.5 or four hours at Versailles, so we just scratched the surface of what there was to see. We did not get to Marie Antoinette's Estate. We did not see the Musical Fountains show. But what we did see was well worth the trip. Our Paris Pass included a "skip the line" feature, but that only allowed us to skip the Ticket Purchasing line. There was still a very long security line you had to go through to get inside the palace after tickets were purchased. But one of the security personnel gave me a tip that I will pass along here. She told us that if we came back at about 4pm (this was on a Friday), there probably would hardly be any length to the security line at that point. Sure enough, we returned there at 4pm, and pretty much were able to walk right through the security checkpoint with no waiting. So, this is a very important tip to keep in mind when doing your Versailles trip-panning!

On the way back to the Train Station, we took our time strolling through the little cluster of souvenir shops that lined one side of the street, to see if we could find any memories. Carol actually found a good deal on a couple of lovely throw pillows, and they now decorate the window-seat in our kitchen.

Friday, June 16th

We had an uneventful trip back to the hotel and arrived there at around 6pm. We decided to take a nap before going out to dinner that night. We had decided to have dinner at an establishment that was just a couple of blocks away, and that had been very highly recommended by our new French friend, Olivier, during the course of our time spent with him and Pim on Carol's birthday.

We woke up at 10pm, freshened up and got dressed, and took the leisurely 10-minute stroll over to the restaurant. It was:

As we entered the premises, we were immediately and surprisingly impressed! First of all, we had to get in a line that was roped off with roping such that you might find in a fine theatre or some such place. We were immediately approached by the dapper Maitre D' who asked how many were in our party. There were probably a dozen or so patrons ahead of us in line. As we waited, we soon got a glimpse of one of the waiters, also impeccably attired with their rondins (tight-fitting black waistcoats) and long white aprons. After about 15 minutes in line, our waiter came and got us and escorted us to our table. Wow! As we passed from the exterior waiting room into the dining hall, we were struck by how large it was, with the very high ceilings, supported by large columns.

We were seated at a long table in the middle of the hall that already had five people sitting on the other half of the table. There was a small, maybe 6-inch high divider separating our half of the table from theirs. The tables were covered with mauve-covered tablecloths, with the Chartier logos on them, and these tablecloths were, in turn, covered by rolls of white paper. As we would soon learn, this paper was where the waiters wrote down your order as you gave it. Anyhow, our new tablemates seemed like a happy bunch and were just laughing and talking away. We soon started chatting with them, and before long, it felt like we were all old friends. They were native French, all probably in their 40's, except for one of the women's mother, who we found out later had recently turned 60.

During our conversation, it came up that we were in Paris to celebrate Carol's birthday, which had been two days ago.

At one point, a couple of our new friends excused themselves to get up to go outside to have a smoke. I noticed one of them stopping to talk to a waitress on her way out. I thought that was nice of them to excuse themselves for the smoke, and I thought it was even nicer that this was apparently a non-smoking establishment.

By this time, the waiter had led another couple to our half of the table, so now we had new friends on both sides of us. This new couple looked like they could have been a young man with his grandmother.

These guys seemed friendly enough, but the real action and fun conversation was being held between us and our new friends, so we politely welcomed these new guys to the table, and got back to our friends.

Corrina and Lorenz had returned from their smoke by now. Corrina was sitting at the end of the table, and she seemed to be the ring-leader, and also the most fun. She spoke almost flawless English, but with a French accent, of course.

By this time, it was about 1:30am, and we had been making merry with Corrina and the gang for about 2 hours now. The restaurant had stopped taking orders at 11:30 and most of the patrons had left, but we were still going strong.

I looked up in the aisle behind Carol and saw a waiter approaching… with a Blazing Cupcake! It was a cupcake that had a giant 4th-of-July like sparkler stuck in it. Now I know why Corrina had stopped to talk to the waiter on her way out.

Carol broke into a big smile as the waiter sat the cupcake in front of her and the guys started singing the Stevie Wonder version of "Happy Birthday", and "Cherish the Love" by Kool & The Gang. It turns out that the reason they had that Kool & The Gang song on their mind is that they had just come from a theatre around the corner where that group had been in concert. I wish I'd known!

Anyhow, shortly after this "Lovefest" was over, Carol and I gave the French double-cheek kiss to all of the women on the way out and we bid Adieu to Corrina and the Gang. It was a little after 2am when we hopped into bed, exhausted again, but looking forward to our last full day in Gay Paris!

Note: When we returned to the States and I started doing my background and research work for this book, I found out some very interesting things about <u>Bouillon Chartier, 7 rue du Fauborg Montmartre 75009</u>). It had originally opened back in 1896 by the Chartier Brothers and it was classified as a Historical Monument of Paris in 1989. The restaurant is beloved by native Parisians, and tourists also flock to it by the droves.

SATURDAY, JUNE 17ᵀᴴ

Monet's Garden at Giverny

We were eagerly looking forward to our last day in Paris, as a day of chilling and relaxation. We had taken the advice of our Mayor and booked the Monet Gardens at Giverny tour before we left the States. Claude Monet was a founder of the French Impressionist movement and one of that movement's most prolific artists. The trip to see the place where he worked and lived for the latter part of his life until his death, would give us an opportunity to see some of the French countryside on a leisurely ride outside of Paris. The tour van was supposed to pick us up right at our hotel door at 8am, and sure enough, we saw him park across the street from the hotel and make his way to the front door shortly after eight.

When we entered the van, there were already two other parties in it. One was an elderly lady, Zora, who was traveling by herself, and was from an island off of one of Canada's western provinces. The other party consisted of a woman, and her two teen-age kids- one boy and one girl -

Saturday, June 17th

from Spokane, Washington. We actually pulled away from the curb at around 8:15 and when we reached Giverny, at the end of a 65-mile trip, it was about 9:30. The trip itself was very relaxing. We got to see some of the French countryside and actually crossed the Seine River, up around Vernon, about 7 kilometers away from Giverny.

Giverny seemed to be a quaint little village and the driver pulled into a parking lot a few blocks after we entered the town. He pointed us to where we could enter the Monet grounds at a "hidden" entranceway to skip the lines, and he told us what time he would be back to pick us up, and we were off. Zora kind of attached herself to Carol and me as our third wheel. We were both cool with that because she was pleasant enough, and we realized that most travel experiences are more enjoyable when you have someone to share them with.

The Monet Gardens consisted of four main areas – the House, the Gardens, the Water Garden, and the Water Lily Pond. Our entry point took us directly into the Gardens, and the aroma in the air smelled as if we were in a perfume factory. I don't know if I have ever seen so many different types and colors of flowers in one location before as I did in these gardens.

Monet actually designed the Garden himself, as a "place to paint in, an open-air studio." But not only did he design the Garden, he also took an active role in actually creating it, often taking to digging, planting, and hoeing with his own hands, while his children had the task of watering.

He was constantly going to-and-fro between his garden studios, where he loved to paint from nature when the weather permitted, and his indoor studios, which he never went to without grumbling, but from which he still got a lot of his work done. Here are just a few samples from the Garden.

Saturday, June 17th

These are my favorite rooms and views in Monet's house.

Monet's Bedroom on 2nd Floor

View from Monet's Bedroom Window

I thought that Monet's bedroom was pretty cool for a couple of reasons. First of all, the view he had out the window, as shown above, was absolutely fantastic. The photo does not do it justice, but I can definitely see how inspiring it would be to wake up each morning and start your day off with that view! I also thought that it was enlightening to discover that Monet did not have any of his own paintings in his bedroom. Instead he filled the walls

Saturday, June 17th

with paintings by some of his friends, most of whom were also Impressionistic masters in their own right. Among these were Boudin, Cailebotte, Cezannes, and the great Renoir. The painting of the naked woman in the top left-hand corner is a Renoir. There was also a painting in there by Berthe Morisot, reportedly the only female artist that he was ever heard to have given any praise to.

One of my other favorite rooms in the house was Monet's Drawing Room on the first floor. Just think of it as kind of a combination den/library, but instead of books, he had paintings – his own paintings – hung everywhere. It was said that he had hung them as sort of a shrine dedicated to his own paintings. He was once quoted as saying, "These are old memories in this room. They matter to me; I like to have them around me. As far as possible… I have kept a painting from every stage of my life." He liked to entertain visiting friends with tales from his life, in the form of commentaries on the paintings he had hung on the walls.

After taking our tour through the house, we headed for the Water Garden and the Water Lily Pond.

We had to go through a tunnel that led under the street to get to this area, which was located on the far side of the property. When we emerged, it was as though we had been transported into some magical land far away. It was beautiful!

Saturday, June 17th

Water Lily Pond with the famous Japanese Bridge in the background.

And this may be my favorite shot...maybe because I'm a fisherman!

This Water Garden and its' Water Lily Pond were the source of much of Monet's inspiration and many of his paintings.

After taking in all of the splendor and serenity of the Water Garden and Water Lily Pond, we decided to go have a bite to eat before our van returned for us, and to take a stroll through Give rny up to the Church Cemetery in which Monet and his family were buried. Zora was still hanging with us, so the three of us exited the grounds and started walking up the narrow street until we came to an outdoor restaurant.

Saturday, June 17th

Having thoroughly enjoyed a wonderful, relaxing morning at Monet's Garden and Giverny and a delicious lunch, we made our way back to the waiting van, where our other van-mates were already happily ensconced, licking on some ice cream cones.

We were dropped off back at our hotel at about 2:30pm. We wanted to take advantage of every moment in this, our last Day in Paris, so we decided to explore our immediate neighborhood a bit more before freshening up and changing for our Last Supper in Paris.

We discovered a couple of little side streets that had some nice clothing and shoe boutiques on them, but as it was Saturday, most of them were closed. We regretted that we had not discovered them earlier in the week. I guess we did not truly appreciate what a great location our hotel was in, with all of the activity in the neighborhood, like bars, restaurants, bakeries, museums, and retail – all within a short walking distance. If we ever return to Paris, I would definitely choose the same hotel to stay in. The combination of location, service, and friendliness of the entire staff, made it a real winner in my book.

We decided to have a rather early dinner – around 8:30 – since we had to get up at around 2:30am in order to be ready for the Super Shuttle that we had reserved to take us to the airport. It was supposed to be at our front door at 3:30am. So, we went back to what had turned out to be our favorite neighborhood hangout, La Porte Montmartre, for our last round of People Watching. As we settled into our seats, we saw our French friends, Olivier and Pim, whom we had met at the same place a few nights earlier. So, they joined us, and we chatted and got to say our final farewells to them. That was a perfect way to end our last night in Paris. So much for the oft-heard saying that the French are unfriendly and rude. We met no such French women or men that fit that description, during our entire trip.

We actually got back to the hotel at a decent hour – 10pm – and settled in for our little four hours of sleep.

SUNDAY, JUNE 18ᵀᴴ

Homeward Bound

03:15 – Super Shuttle arrives.

I was sitting in the lobby when the big black van pulled up 15 minutes early. Carol was not down yet, as she had to put on the finishing touches, as women are prone to do.

It was 3:30 on the dot, when Carol finally got down to the lobby. The driver and I had already loaded our luggage into the van, so we walked across the street, he opened the door, and we got in. We were the first of his pickups on the way back to the airport.

The first thing I noticed as we settled in, was that there was still a lot of loud noise and music coming from the club that was about half-a-block and right around the corner from our hotel. As we wove through the streets of Paris, we passed many clubs and restaurants, and the scene was pretty much the same in all of them – people sitting at the outdoor tables people-watching, or spillover crowds from inside standing outside the bar or café, talking loud with a cigarette or drink in their hand. Paris is truly "The City That Never Sleeps!"

We made our last stop and picked up the final passenger, and we were off to Charles de Gaulle. This last lady lived on a street not too far from the Champs-Elysees, and shortly after she plopped in, we turned onto that magnificent boulevard and the Arc de Triomphe came into view. What a sight; our last viewing of another historic monument. *The very next day, after we returned home, we would see the view of the Arc from almost this exact same vantage point, as CNN ran footage of where an alleged terrorist had driven his car into a police car- less than 24 hours after we were in that same spot. He was killed at the scene by the police. That was too close!*

At Charles de Gaulle (CDG) Airport

Our short stay at CDG was not without drama. The plane was about 30-minutes late taking off for our 55-minute flight to Brussels, Belgium. The pilot made up some of that time, but that still made it a little tight catching our connection in Brussels.

Brussels (BRU) Airport

Brussels airport was Huge; much bigger than I would have imagined. We came into the A Terminal and had to go over to the C, and there was a vast shopping area in the terminal between those two. It had dozens of stores, and not just your typical airport stores either. If one did not know better, you might think you were in a mall. Since we were in Belgium, I figured there would be no better place to get some Belgian Chocolates, so I stopped at one of the fancy candy stores and purchased a large box.

Sunday, June 18th

For all of you Football (Soccer) fans out there, we saw the Manchester United Football club's private plane parked at the Brussels Airport, so here's a quick glimpse of it, just for you!

When we got to our gate and it was time for boarding, we had to go through another security check that was right past the ticket counter, and right before the hallway that led to the aircraft. I went through with no problem, but as luck (bad) would have it, Carol got flagged for one of the random thorough checks. I settled into a seat on one of the leather sofas in the hallway to wait for her. The lucky "chosen ones" were herded to an area behind a folding partition, so the security agents could do their thing.

I waited and waited and waited and waited, and finally, after what seemed like close to an hour, she came through. Good thing we did not have a tight timeframe for our flight to Dulles!

Dulles Airport (IAD) – Washington, DC

After our 8-hour and 40-minute flight across the Atlantic, we landed at Dulles almost exactly at the time we were scheduled to arrive. Timeliness was really not a concern here though, as we had a 4.5-hour layover ahead of us. On the way from our arrival gate to the departure gate, I peeked into one of the news and magazine stores that we passed and saw that they had a Presidential Podium at the back of the store with a life-size cutout of Trump behind it, with his wife Melania off to the side. I asked the woman behind the counter if I could take a photo behind the podium, and she said Sure. I just told her to be sure and get Trump completely out of the way!

I'm sure I could make just as good a President as 45, and I am much better looking - LOL!

Dallas – Fort Worth International Airport
(Good old DFW)

Well, after about 13 hours in the air from the time we left Paris, and about 19.5 hours overall, we finally touched down at DFW at 7:49pm Sunday night, June 18th, right on schedule! There's NO place like home, no matter where you may roam. It felt great when we touched down on US soil back at Dulles, but it felt extra-great to be back on our Home Turf!

When we got to the Baggage Claim area to get our bags, our daughter Sue and granddaughter, Mia were there waiting for us by the Baggage Carousels. Now we were REALLY Home!!!

WRAP-UP

Well, that's it. I sincerely hope that you enjoyed reading this book as much as I did writing it and reliving our Paris excursion. Paris is truly one of the world's Great Cities! The energy in that city is amazing, and it is one of the few cities in the world that I have been to that I would go back to over and over again, given the opportunity. New York City, specifically Manhattan, is another vibrant city that comes to mind. And Bangkok, although it has a definitely different, definitely Asian vibe, also is a city with the kind of vitality that keeps drawing you back. I would be remiss if I did not also include my hometown of Chicago on that list (I grew up in East Chicago, Indiana, 25 miles from downtown Chicago, but I still claim it). But Paris is at the top of that list, in my humble opinion, when you consider the history, the architecture, the food, the Arts, and the people. There are still many major cities on the world-stage that I have not traveled to, but one day…

I DID mention the food, didn't I? We had some excellent meals in Paris, and I must say that everything I ate was good, with some meals being sublime. So, I wanted to share with you some recipes of some of the entrees that we feasted on. I know that Carol and I will definitely be in the kitchen trying some of these out soon.

So, let me leave you with that. Again, I hope you came away with some travel tips, and got a little enjoyment as well from tagging along with us. See you next time!

APPENDIX A

RECIPES

I have included a few recipes in this section, all of which were entrees or deserts that we feasted on while in Paris. I am listing each dish under the heading of the restaurant in which we dined upon it at. I actually gathered the recipes after returning to the States, so they may not be prepared exactly as they were at the restaurant. But I believe they should be close enough to give you a feel (or taste) of what our dining experiences were like over in Paris. Heck, if you guys don't want to try these out for yourselves, I've got a sneaking suspicion that I may be doing so!!

Bon Appetit!!!

APPENDIX A

At Au Cadet de Gascogne:

Artists Square – Page 49

1. Magret de Canard
2. Penne Bolognese

How to make France's 'most-loved' dish - Magret de Canard

Magret de Canard is duck breast from the Moulard (*Mulard*, in French) breed of ducks. The Moulard is a cross between the White Pekin and the Muscovy duck

Ingredients:

2 Magrets de Canard

Juice from 2 oranges

1 orange sliced and peeled

3 tbsp of sugar

¼ cup of Cointreau

Salt and pepper

Method:
1. Clean the Magrets de Canard.
2. With a sharp knife remove the two white membranes so the Magrets will not curl when cooking.
3. Trim the fat from the side and carve the top of the skin in diamond shapes
4. Place the Magrets de Canard to cook on medium heat, skin side down. No fat is needed as the fat from the skin will melt straight away.
5. Let it cook for 10 minutes then turn. If too much fat has melted, remove it from the pan.
6. Make sure the meat is well seared everywhere.
7. Remove the Magrets and place them on a plate covered with aluminum foil.
8. Remove all the fat from the pan, but do not clean it.
9. Deglaze the pan with the orange juice.
10. Add the sugar, orange slices and Cointreau. Cook until the juices are caramelized, about 10 minutes at medium heat.
11. Add the Magrets back to the pan and let it cook for another 10 minutes basting them with the juices.
12. When the Magrets de Canard are ready, let them rest for 5 minutes

Then slice them and pour the juices on top.
1. You can serve it with a gratin dauphinoise and vegetables of your choice.

PENNE BOLOGNESE

Ingredients:

¼ cup olive oil

6 cloves garlic, finely chopped

1 medium carrot, finely chopped

1 stalk celery, finely chopped

1 small yellow onion, finely chopped

½ tsp. crushed red chile flakes

½ lb. ground veal

¼ lb. ground pork

Kosher salt and freshly ground black pepper, to taste

2 tbsp. tomato paste

½ cup dry red wine

1 28-oz. can whole peeled tomatoes in juice, crushed

10 fresh basil leaves, roughly chopped

2 sprigs fresh thyme

1 bay leaf

1 lb. dried penne rigate or ziti

Grated parmesan, for serving

Instructions:

Heat oil in an 8-qt. saucepan over medium-high heat. Add garlic, carrots, celery, onions, and chile flakes, and cook until golden, 8 to 10 minutes. Add veal, pork, salt and pepper; cook, stirring and breaking up meat, until meat is browned, about 8 minutes. Add tomato paste and cook, stirring, until browned, about 2 minutes. Add wine and cook until reduced by half, about 3 minutes. Add tomatoes, basil, thyme, and bay leaf. Simmer, stirring occasionally, until sauce is thick, about 6 minutes more.

Meanwhile, bring a large pot of salted water to a boil over high heat. Add penne and cook until al dente, about 8 minutes. Drain, reserving $\frac{1}{2}$ cup pasta water. Toss pasta with sauce and reserved water. Serve with grated Parmesan.

Serves 6 – 8.

APPENDIX A

At La Porte Montmartre

Carol's Birthday Dinner

Page 86

1. Duck Confit with Baby Potatoes
2. Veal Brawn with Gribiche Sauce

DUCK CONFIT

Duck confit is considered one of the finest French dishes. While it is made across France, it is seen as a specialty of Gascony. The **confit** is prepared in a centuries-old process of preservation that consists of salt curing a piece of meat (generally goose duck, or pork) and then cooking it in its own fat.

Once esteemed as a preservation method, cooking and keeping duck in its rendered fat results in meltingly tender, moist, and extremely flavorful meat which can be used in a variety of simple preparations. Sear the duck legs in a hot skillet or shred the meat and add it to salads, or, perhaps best of all, make duck rillettes. Just remember the duck must be salted a day before you plan to cook it.

Ingredients

- 3 tablespoons salt
- 4 cloves garlic, smashed
- 1 shallot, peeled and sliced
- 6 sprigs thyme
- Coarsely ground black pepper
- 4 duck legs with thighs
- 4 duck wings, trimmed
- About 4 cups duck fat

Preparation

1. Sprinkle 1 tablespoon of salt in the bottom of a dish or plastic container large enough to hold the duck pieces in a single layer. Evenly scatter half the garlic, shallots, and thyme in the container. Arrange the duck, skin-side up, over the salt mixture, then sprinkle with the remaining salt, garlic, shallots, and thyme and a little pepper. Cover and refrigerate for 1-2 days.

2. Preheat the oven to 225°F. Melt the duck fat in a small saucepan. Brush the salt and seasonings off the duck. Arrange the duck pieces in a single snug layer in a high-sided baking dish or ovenproof saucepan. Pour the melted fat over the duck (the duck pieces should be covered by fat)

and place the confit in the oven. Cook the confit slowly at a very slow simmer — just an occasional bubble — until the duck is tender and can be easily pulled from the bone, 2-3 hours. Remove the confit from the oven. Cool and store the duck in the fat. (The confit will keep in the refrigerator for several weeks.)

Note:
The duck fat can be strained, cooled and reused.

Veal Shank With Sauce Gribiche

Ingredients

- 1 veal shank, 4 pounds
- 1 clove garlic
- 3 quarts water
- 2 cups coarsely chopped onions
- 1 cup trimmed, scraped coarsely chopped carrots
- 12 peppercorns
- 1 bay leaf
- ½ teaspoon dried thyme
- 2 whole cloves
- 4 sprigs fresh parsley
- Sauce gribiche (see recipe)

Preparation

1. Make 8 gashes in veal shank. Cut garlic into 8 thin slices and insert.

2. Put shanks in kettle and add all remaining ingredients except sauce. Bring to boil and cover. Let simmer about 2 1/2 hours.

3. Remove shank and strain cooking liquid, discarding solids. Slice meat and serve with sauce gribiche. Reserve broth for future use.

At La Fontaine de Mars
The "Obama" Restaurant

Pages 99

1. *Canette* (Roast Duckling Fillet with sauce and wine-poached dates)
2. *Bar Aux Olives* (Rosemary Roast with Olives)

Pan-Roasted Duck Breasts with Onions and Crisp Pancetta

Ingredients

- 2 red onions, sliced 1/2 inch thick
- 1/4 cup extra-virgin olive oil
- 2 thyme sprigs
- 8 sage leaves

- Four 6-ounce Pekin duck breasts
- Kosher salt and freshly ground pepper
- 1/2 pound thinly sliced pancetta
- 1 garlic clove, minced

How to Make It

Step 1

Preheat the oven to 450°. In a large bowl, separate the onion rings and toss with 2 tablespoons of the oil, the thyme and sage. Spread the onions out on a large baking sheet and roast for about 20 minutes, tossing once, until tender and golden. Leave the oven on.

Step 2

Meanwhile, score the fat on the duck in a crosshatch pattern; season the duck with salt and pepper. Heat a large ovenproof skillet. Add the duck, skin side down, and cook over moderate heat until the skin is golden brown, about 7 minutes. Turn the duck and roast in the oven for about 6 minutes for medium rare. Transfer the duck to a cutting board and let rest for 5 minutes.

Step 3

Add the pancetta to the skillet and cook over moderate heat until browned and crisp, about 5 minutes; drain on paper towels. Pour off all but 2 tablespoons of the fat from the skillet. Add the garlic to the skillet and cook over high heat until fragrant but not browned, about 1 minute. Add the demiglace and vinegar and bring to a boil, scraping up any browned bits. Remove the skillet from the heat; whisk in the walnut oil and the remaining 2 tablespoons of olive oil and season the dressing with salt and pepper.

Step 4

Arrange the baby greens and roasted onions on 4 large plates and drizzle with some of the dressing. Thinly slice the duck breasts crosswise and arrange over the salads. Drizzle the remaining dressing on top, garnish with the pancetta and serve.

APPENDIX A

Rosemary Roast with Fennell and Green Olives

Ingredients

- 3 tablespoons chopped fresh rosemary leaves
- 2 tablespoons minced garlic
- 1 boned pork loin roast (about 3 lbs.), strings removed, rinsed, and dried
- Kosher salt
- Pepper
- 1/3 pound thinly sliced prosciutto
- 2 tablespoons olive oil
- 3 pounds fresh fennel, bulbs stemmed, cored, and cut into wedges, plus 1/2 cup chopped fronds
- 2 cups dry white wine
- 1 cup pitted green olives, halved

How to Make It

Step 1

Preheat oven to 350°. Mix rosemary and garlic in a small bowl. Sprinkle one side of roast lightly with salt and pepper. Spread with half the rosemary-garlic mixture, pressing it on. Drape half the prosciutto lengthwise over loin. Holding the prosciutto on the roast, turn it over. Sprinkle with more salt and pepper, spread remaining rosemary mixture over the top, and drape with remaining prosciutto. Tie roast at 1 1/2-in. intervals with heavy cotton string, tucking prosciutto into place.

Step 2

Pour oil into a large frying pan over medium-high heat. Add roast and cook until prosciutto is crisp and beginning to brown on the bottom. Turn roast and cook until other side is crisp and browned, about 5 minutes total. Transfer to a plate.

Step 3

Add fennel bulbs to frying pan and cook, stirring often, until beginning to brown, about 5 minutes. Spread in a large roasting pan. Add wine to frying pan and bring to a boil, stirring to scrape up browned bits. Pour over fennel. Set pork loin on top.

Step 4

Bake until a thermometer inserted in the center of roast reaches 135° for medium, about 45 minutes. Transfer roast to a board and let rest in a warm place 15 minutes (temperature will rise to 140°).

Step 5

Meanwhile, set roasting pan over 2 burners on high heat, and cook, stirring often, until liquid is almost evaporated, 5 to 10 minutes. Remove from heat and stir in olives and fennel fronds.

Step 6

Cut string from roast, slice, and serve with fennel mixture.

APPENDIX B

Bonus Photos

This appendix contains Street Artist's drawings of me done on this vacation trip to Paris and from my earlier visits to Paris in 1977 and 1997.

In 1977, I was in the US Air Force, stationed in Bitburg, Germany, and some of my friends and I had gone over to Paris to celebrate the coming in of 1977. In 1997, I was on a business trip with the semiconductor company I worked for, rolling out upgraded computer systems in our offices in Paris, Munich, Milan, and Reading, England. Looks like it must be my fate/destiny to be in Paris every 20 years. Looking forward to 2037 to see what the 82-year-old me will look like!

STREET ARTIST DRAWING OF THE AUTHOR — JUNE 2017

Montmartre

STREET ARTIST DRAWING OF THE AUTHOR — 1997

Montmartre

APPENDIX B

STREET ARTIST DRAWING OF THE AUTHOR — NEW YEAR'S DAY, 1977

Montmartre

ABOUT THE AUTHOR

Warren Landrum

Warren G. Landrum, Jr. was born in East Chicago, Indiana. He went off to college to Purdue University, from which he graduated with a degree in Information Systems and Computer Programming. He later received a B.S. in Management from the University of Phoenix.

Warren served in the U.S. Air Force, both at home and abroad. It was during that time that he first became exposed to overseas travel, a passion that he would pursue at every opportunity. While stationed in Germany, he was able to travel throughout Europe, experiencing the various cultures and lifestyles in Holland, Switzerland, France, Luxembourg, Belgium, and England.

ABOUT THE AUTHOR

Warren continued his traveling ways upon entering corporate America. He had assignments in Bermuda, Taiwan, Bangkok, Thailand (12 trips); and back to Europe again, this time experiencing Paris, Milan, Munich, and the London-Reading area. All of those experiences, along with his leisure travel to various parts of Mexico, Canada, The Caribbean, and throughout the US, along with being married to a Jamaican wife, have truly given Warren a global perspective and insight in regards to both observing and living life!!

Warren's other passions are fishing, which he inherited as part of the Landrum gene-pool/DNA, basketball, and performing as a singer. He founded the Sun Valley Revue, a sextet of talented singer/entertainers that performed 'old-school' R&B music for around two years in the Phoenix area in the late 1990's.

Warren is also the author of four books that have been published - "The Heart & Soul of a Black Man;" "Let's Go Home to Indiana Harbor: Reflections From Mid-Town America;" "Texas Politics – Grand Prairie Style: Campaign 2013;" "The Stroke of Grace: Trauma, Triumph and Testimony of Former NBA Player Juaquin "Hawk" Hawkins," which he co-wrote with Mr. Hawkins; and the latest one, "Nine Days in Italy: The Highs and Lows of Driving Through Italia."

Warren works as a Systems Engineer for Baylor, Scott & White Healthcare and has been an IT professional for about 34 years.

In the area of Civic involvement, he ran for City Council in Grand Prairie in 2013 and is also currently Chairman of the Library Board for the city, a member of the

Rotary Club and a past Grand Prairie YMCA Board member. He is also a member of the Mayor's Roundtable, a select group of citizens hand-picked by the Mayor, who meet periodically with the Mayor to advise him on issues and needs of the citizenry, in addition to making suggestions that can serve to benefit the city, if and when implemented.

Warren is a member of Alpha Phi Alpha Fraternity, Inc., the first Black Greek Letter Fraternity.

Warren and his beautiful wife Carol recently celebrated their 29th Wedding Anniversary and are the proud parents of one daughter, Suzette, and a three-year old granddaughter – Mia.

www.ingramcontent.com/pod-product-compliance
Lightning Source LLC
Chambersburg PA
CBHW040321300426
44112CB00020B/2832